aflame books

Halala Madiba
Nelson Mandela in Poetry

Edited by Richard Bartlett
Consulting Editor: Morakabe Seakhoa

Foreword by Nadine Gordimer
Preface by Andries Oliphant

Aflame Books
2 The Green
Laverstock
Wiltshire
SP1 1QS
United Kingdom
email: info@aflamebooks.com

First published in 2006 by Aflame Books

The editor and publishers of this book have made considerable efforts to contact all rights holders, whether the poets themselves or their publishers. This has been difficult in some cases: poets are deceased and their heirs are untraceable; publishing houses have ceased to exist or have merged; poets have moved and their whereabouts are unknown. The editor and publishers wish sincerely to thank all those who granted permission and all those who assisted in our search by providing leads. We welcome any further information that anyone is able to provide.

ISBN: 0-9552339-0-9
EAN: 978-0-9552339-0-6

Cover design by Geraldine Hendler (geraldine.hendler@gmail.com)
Typesetting and layout by Richard Bartlett

Printed by Main Choice International Development, Hong Kong

To our children,
and all the children of South Africa
for whom this story is nothing
more than history

Note: Reading of poetry can be influenced by the way it is visually structured, and in an effort to preserve this tangible aspect of the art, each page, as far as possible, marks the beginning of a new stanza or line sequence. The end of a poem is marked by _____ .

Words or phrases that may be unfamiliar to readers are explained in a Glossary on Page 280.

Thanks are due to many people who helped in bringing this project to fruition: Raks Seakhoa whose friendship and professionalism made so much possible; all those contributors who went out of their way to assist us in tracking down some hard-to-find works; Luzette Strauss, my partner in life and work, for her undying support and sharp eyes; to translators and critics Luís Mitras, Mike Dewar, Menzi Ndaba, Ann Reckless, Mandlakayise Matyumza and Vusi Mchuni; to Rowena Dewar for making her language skills available to us; to Graham Addison for making his graphic design facilities available; the Poetry Library, based in London, whose database was a most useful resource and efficiently provided despite major building works; and Geraldine Hendler for ensuring that the cover does justice to the contents despite impossible deadlines.

A list of acknowledgements for poems included is on Page 295.

Table of Contents

Foreword

How does one define greatness? There are two main categories, surely. There is intellectual greatness. There is the greatness of the individual human spirit in activity of body and mind down among fellow human beings: the greatness of total courage in commitment to attainment of freedom – for everyone; freedom by definition knows no boundaries.

Looking back at the century we have so recently left behind, there are two men whose greatness stands out, and forever. Mahatma Gandhi is dead; his inspiration is not. Nelson Mandela is with us, inspiration for the struggle of the past, inspiration for the present, for the future.

An anthology of poetry dedicated to him, not by a few lines preceding the contents, but inherent in the works of the poets themselves, transformed expressions of a pervading, deep consciousness of the meaning of a great presence invigorating our lives, was an idea waiting to happen. Richard Bartlett and Morakabe Seakhoa have taken it up boldly, innovatively, on the principle well asserted by lines from one of the contributing poets, Maxamed Xaashi Dhamac: 'poetry has the strength/To tell the story well'.

Why poetry rather than prose? What is there that the biography and even autobiography cannot tell, of greatness? Poetry, the highest literary form of the gift of intense imaginative identity with the subject, goes beyond the objective and subjective with the prescience of something almost like an act of faith. Faith that the truth of the great man or woman lies somewhere to be expressed, in between, and in synthesis with the complexities of what the great individual has meant, and means, with the consciousness and subconscious of others. This goes beyond influence in the ordinary sense of the term, does not depend necessarily on contact with the great one, even with sharing the same conflict and conditions, the same country.

The poems in this book come from South Africa, yes, but also from all over the world, the USA, Ireland, England and other countries, some are translated from French, Portuguese, Somali. The phrase 'A Man of The World' usually denotes someone sophisticated, aware of this wide context but debonairly detached from commitment to any particular country or politics. There is quite another definition remarkably evidenced in the origins of the poetry gathered in this collection. Mandela is a Man of The World in this other sense. The real, the vital one, the shouldering of huge human responsibility, far beyond the personal. He is often described admiringly, but mistakenly, now, as an icon. But he is not, even cast within the reverence of old age, a figure on a pedestal, in a niche or as depicted in a shopping mall square in Johannesburg, a bronze giant. He continues to be a living and highly vocal proponent of not just the ideas, but vehemently the practical implementation of what people worldwide recognise in themselves and their societies, as wanting in their political formations, their health and other social services, their right to free speech. His words have become a litmus by which others can test the authenticity of justice, free of cant. And he shows it is a moral condition that one must not be afraid to criticise when wrongs are committed in one's own country by one's own political formation.

The poems in this collection confirm all Mandela has been and is, his relevance at home in South Africa and to a world where conflict proliferates, with analogies to the long historical one that, without him to lead us, would not have been overcome. Mongane Wally Serote's poem 'History is the Home Address' brings poetry's succinct beauty to sum up what has come about. Mandela provides the unmatched guidance of his historically hard-earned wisdom to the outside world, from home in our country, where it all happened.

There is much enjoyment as well as thoughtful stimulation in the book. Inevitably, some of the poems fall into the cliché mode with verbal toyi-toyi, worn slogans of the past. But most, particularly those that come out of what Dennis Brutus names a 'barred' existence, in his poem 'Robben Island', have their own powerful, individual voice that echoes strikingly after the poem is read. For *Halala Madiba*, as Mandela would be the first to insist, is not about Mandela; it is about all who have lived through and are living in his times, in South Africa and, as we have come to realise, the times of the world. The Irish Nobel Prize poet, Seamus Heaney, promises for the present "...someone is hearing/The outcry and the birth-cry/Of new life.../It means once in a lifetime/That justice can rise up/And hope and history rhyme'. Mandela's daughter Zindzi writes movingly and with originality to her 'Tata'. There's delightful humour in the West-Indian English of Benjamin Zephaniah's satirical poem taking on those who with hasty pragmatism changed sides after 1994: 'Nobody done apartheid/Dey were all revolutionaries'.

Everyone who reads this anthology will have a favourite poem. I have hope that the pleasureful revelation of rewards to be found in poetry may mean that this bold venture into publication will find the wide readership it deserves and encourage publishers to think again about their reluctance to take on the work of poets. It cannot be left to 'performance' poets to keep the ancient art alive; often the poem has no life to it without the physical medium of the poet's body and voice. We need books like this generous one, to take in our hands and return to, when alone.

Nadine Gordimer
Johannesburg, February 2006

Preface

I imagine that many readers will pick up this book of poems inspired by the life of Nelson Mandela with a sense of discovery. I could of course be mistaken. Nevertheless, I presume that this sense of discovery, both in South Africa and beyond, will be triggered by the fact that a great deal has been written about Nelson Mandela over the last 50 years or so. A world figure even during his long incarceration, his face and name as well as his life-story have been disseminated in a multitude of languages to all corners of the world. Yet, I have a hunch that outside certain literary circles across the globe few among the general public know that a vast body of poems inspired by his life is extant in many languages of the world.

Commencing in the early 1960s, this poetry with Mandela and South Africa as its subject peaked during the 1980s and 1990s. Poems in this tradition, as this publication indicates, are still being written now. It can be expected that more will be written in the near future. In fact, as future poets learn about Mandela's life and the history of South Africa, they too are likely to be moved to reaffirm its significance. Composed from what are now unforeseeable future developments, the inspiration they will find in his example, will not be in any effort to further immortalise him but rather to invoke his name and to interpret his life and the history of South Africa to counteract the pernicious tendency of history to repeat itself, in South Africa or elsewhere, either as tragedy or as farce.

While this is not the first book of poems dedicated to Mandela, this anthology is distinctive in so far as it gathers poems written over half a century by poets from many different countries and covers both his time in prison and the one and a half decades since his release. Other books of this kind are either limited to one country or compiled to coincide with a specific historical moment. Most are mainly concerned with the period of his imprisonment. As such, this anthology provides a comprehensive perspective on the poetry in which Mandela and South Africa feature.

What will strike the reader of this book, then, is that amid the clamour and violent upheavals of the 20th century and during the long silence which was imposed on Mandela through his imprisonment, poets in South Africa and elsewhere found a subject in the life of one man. This enabled them to assume unabashed public voices in a range of poetic modalities when the reigning aesthetics in parts of what was the self-declared "free world" decreed that poetry belonged to the spheres of the private, intimate and subjective. Elsewhere, in the self proclaimed "socialist world", disdain of all forms of privacy and subjectivity saw to it that poetry was dragooned into translating state ideologies into verse. Between these wastelands, in the complex terrain located between these reductive polarities, Mandela emerged as a subject which generated an alternative poetic register in South Africa and other parts of the world. In this register, private and public perspectives were not sundered from each other but were explored simultaneously. This, as can be read in this collection, was done by focusing on an individual's fate within a specific social and political matrix and by exploring the ways in which individual actions may direct, coincide with or run against prevailing establishments.

By exploring the specific human situation and all its broader ramifications, this writing broke out of the paralysis imposed by aesthetic prescriptions calling either for the expunction of politics from poetry or the endorsement of rearticulating the crudities of a depersonalised aesthetics governed by ideological instrumentality. In this collection the reader will be able to traverse a much richer spectrum of poetic modalities than any fixed tradition allows for. More significantly perhaps, the reader can enjoy a wide range of poetic talents, each grounded in its own sense of what is worthy of poetic treatment.

In many instances the writing arose from profound identifications with Mandela. This occurred regardless of the distance between the poets and their subject, who, after all, was shut away from the world. Nevertheless, from their respective privacies and social affiliations, poets strove to symbolically breach the isolation and unbearable negation of freedom endured by Mandela for so long. In other instances the poetry issued from direct contact with Mandela, either as fellow prisoners on Robben Island or as his associates before his arrest. Through imaginative projection and from experience the diverse corpus of poetry thematising Mandela was fashioned.

Generally speaking, the poetry collected in this publication, deals with what poets either knew or imagined were the conditions of his imprisonment, his ideals and their implication for South Africa and the world. Because of this most of the poems are suffused with admiration for the man. In others such as Wole Soyinka's 'Your Logic Frightens Me, Mandela' this admiration is underscored even as questions are posed with regard to the extent to which Mandela's personal sacrifices have been translated into the kind of society and world he declared himself resolved to fight for and, if necessary, to lay down his life pursuing. The bulk of the poems, however, take his life example as a lodestar for the kind of resolve, personal sacrifice and integrity required in times of social and political crisis.

When more closely scrutinised, a specific irony, applicable to the collection as a whole, can be read in some of the poems. For instance, Gerrit Fourie's 'Rivonia': whether read ironically or literally, or in both modes, it articulates the kind of vilification which was used to justify the arrest of Mandela and his associates as well as the suppression of the liberation movement which they led. In this poem Mandela and his fellow revolutionaries are dismissed as nothing more than a regrettable chapter in the reprehensible history of brutality and hatred of would-be revolutionaries, and best forgotten. In place of their cause, the poem invokes "love and peace that conquer". Contrasted with José Craveirinha's 'Ever Since My Friend Nelson Mandela Went to Live on Robben Island', this negative picture is overturned in a gesture of deft irony. For Craveirinha it is not Mandela who was imprisoned but the white minority government and its supporters who shackled themselves to a historical dead-end. It is predicted that Mandela will one day grant them amnesty for their crimes. Between these two extremes of condemnation and an ironic foretelling of the reconciliatory attitude Mandela would adopt upon his release, the poems in this collection range widely to construct images and views on a crucial and heroic figure in South African history.

The fact that he has been singled out for lionisation has as much to do with the trajectory of his life as an individual as with the social and political history of South Africa. From the mid-20th century onwards, Mandela's life and destiny are intertwined with this history. Rooted in the early resistance to colonial conquest, his predecessors include the Khoekoe leader of some of the earliest inhabitants of South Africa. They, like Aushumato and later leaders such as Makana and others from the Eastern Cape, where Mandela was born, were imprisoned by colonial authorities on Robben Island since the 17th century right up to 1994. Some history of this is invoked in Nogqaza we Jojo's 'Ah! Rolihlahla!' and Mongane Wally Serote's 'History is the Home Address'.

South Africa has featured in the global imagination since it, along with the Americas and Asia was drawn into the orbit of an expanding Europe some five centuries ago. This inaugurated the long and arduous passage from colonialism to liberation in which South Africa came to be seen as a particularly fraught manifestation of the contradictions produced by the post Renaissance world system initiated by European expansion. Mandela was destined to lead South Africa to the historical closure of modern colonialism in Africa. Thus when the moment of South Africa's unshackling arrived the world was watching.

At the centre of this, Mandela's entry into poetry via politics and history is therefore not surprising. He is both person and metaphor, a form of metonymy and a symbol in so far as he represented both himself, a society and its oppressed people. This associative relationship between the individual's suffering, endurance, courage and hopes and those of a society lies at the heart of Mandela's meaning for many. This was grasped by poets, as Sipho Sepamla's 'Can I Get a Witness Here' makes clear. It articulates how a man locked away from the world was afoot in France in 1989:

> How can I make everyone believe
> That the streets are full of you
> In Grenoble outside the gates of Pollsmoor prison
> Father Mandela

In reality, however, Mandela was a prisoner. First on the bleak windswept outcrop in the southern Atlantic called Robben Island, then in Pollsmoor Prison in the Cape Peninsula and later further inland in the Western Cape. Since he spent most of his time on Robben Island, it came to represent the iconic universe of his imprisonment. Thus the collection opens with Dennis Brutus's poem which captures the mood of the penal colony. This sets the stage for many poems which deal with the physical and emotional realities of prison life on the island. Today the island is a place of pilgrimage and a point from which the beginnings and the end of colonialism can be read in the landscape of isolation and banishment on the one hand and other of endurance and triumph on the other.

Some of this contradictory complexity is inscribed in Zindzi Mandela's poem to her father 'Ode to My Father'. Addressing her father and posing a series of imaginary statements which seem to take on the form of oblique questions, she writes:

I can imagine

> what you would admire
> if I was disgusted
> what would you love
> if I only hated

Indeed. What capacity for reconciliation would have remained if Mandela and his fellow prisoners allowed themselves to be blighted by blind prejudice and hatred? This poem and all the others collected here enable one to grasp the intricate play of meanings ranging from the personal to the political which poets from all over the world discovered in their subject.

This publication, therefore, is a homage to Mandela and to the poets. It is also a salutation to the peoples of South Africa and the world for whom the liberation of South Africa meant harnessing all human resources, including poetry. Imagine a world thus focused to poetically and practically combine to combat injustice wherever it may exist now and in future. Among the many meanings readers will make of the poems in this collection, for me the poetic record of the long journey from oppression to freedom inscribed on these pages with reference to one person symbolically affirms the significance of every human life.

Andries Oliphant

Pretoria, January 2006

Introduction

Our greatest fear is not that we are inadequate,
but that we are powerful beyond measure.

When Nelson Mandela opened South Africa's first democratic parliament, he did so with a poem. 'Our Greatest Fear' by Marianne Williamson has since come to be associated with Mandela, and he is often thought of as its author. In using a poem for such a momentous occasion Mandela was not merely bringing a new attitude to a formerly "whites-only" institution; he was also implicitly acknowledging the role of poetry in political debate in a country where much poetry, and many of its creators, had been banned for being daring enough to speak out against the best interests of the state. The recital of poetry from within the bastion of the new democratic state in Cape Town in 1994 highlighted both the political possibilities of poetry and Mandela's continuing belief in inclusive, egalitarian politics. This anthology incorporates both of these ideas while paying tribute to the man and to those who took up the pen in his defence.

First conceived when Mandela was a prisoner in Pollsmoor and P.W. Botha was president of South Africa, this project was inspired by the concept of one man as rightful leader of South Africa's people, but was driven by a belief that political consensus and change is driven not by grandiloquence and a belief in inherent superiority but, rather, by numerous small gestures of passionate creativity. This book is one such gesture, made possible thanks to similar gestures by a generation of poets from around the world. That it took more than ten years from conception to production is not a reflection of the complexity of the task, but of the nature of the changing times as the call to "Free Mandela" became redundant and all attention turned to the creation of a new country. The changed political environment led a new outburst of creativity in South Africa and poets around the world also turned their attention to Mandela in his new role as leader, not prisoner. This collection has also therefore become a reflection of the poetry about Mandela that has been published since South Africa became a democracy in 1994.

The relation between politics and poetry, which this collection implicitly depends on, is never an easy one, and art is often transformed into sloganeering behind a façade of poetry. While a few such works are included here, the poems selected were chosen not just because they mentioned Mandela, but also because they offer readers a challenge, a use of language and image, beyond mere sloganeering. All those poets who crafted "Free Mandela" into their art were part of a wider movement and all the poems collected here combine to create a narrative of the struggle to free, not just one man, but all South Africans. For this anthology is not about one man. It is inspired by the life of one of the world's most famous political prisoners, but it tells the story of a whole country and those who supported its fight for justice.

While the collection was initially intended as political statement, it appears now as a historical document recording how Nelson Mandela, in the prison of Robben Island, came to be held up as a symbol of all political prisoners, as an icon in the struggle against apartheid and, more recently, as a symbol of hope and of South Africa's achievements in establishing a vibrant and successful democracy. It is unusual to consider poetry as a tool for relating history or attempting to construct a narrative but the story of Mandela and his country offers a unique opportunity to view the transformation of political expression in art. Collected here is 50 years of poetry on a single, fairly narrow issue of political significance to Africa – and the wider world. If this history is read as poetry and, simultaneously, this poetry is read as history, it offers a view of the ambiguity of poetry as more than fiction and less than history. It also allows an alternative route to understanding and appreciating history not merely as sequence of facts sorted by the prism of politics, but also as emotional endeavour formulated by myriad individuals who act, not as victims or products of history, but as creators of it in seemingly insignificant ways.

Nelson Mandela is central to this book, but it is not a hagiography and it is not just praise poetry. Praise poems are included and it is easy to perceive the collection as little else, considering the eminence of the man, the role he holds as elder statesman and his status in popular imagination. Even the title, *Halala Madiba*, which can be roughly translated as "Praise be to Madiba" (his clan name and the name by which he is affectionately known in South Africa) is one of hagiographic portent. Yet many of the poems collected here are not about him; they are, rather, about what he once represented, and about how that has changed and how he continues to inspire people around the world. Poems included in this anthology were chosen not only because they praise Mandela – they were chosen to map the history of South Africa with Mandela as inspiration. Mandela is almost coincidental to many of the poems in this anthology, yet the frequency with which his name was mentioned, the significance attached to it and the calls for his release all combine to transform the process of naming into a form of resistance, a sign of support for and belief in the principles which Mandela embraces.

Nelson Mandela, together with six fellow revolutionaries, began his life sentence on Robben Island in 1963 after having been convicted for planning armed insurrection against the apartheid state (two others convicted at the same time were not sent to the island because prisons were segregated according to race). Dennis Brutus was already a prisoner on Robben Island when Mandela arrived there, and his poem, which opens this anthology, offers a snapshot of the seemingly hopeless endlessness of the situation in which the African National Congress (ANC) leader and his fellow prisoners found themselves.

Calls for his release came in the immediate aftermath of the Rivonia trial, with Hamish Henderson's 1964 song 'Rivonia' but one example. In his autobiography, Mandela, with wry observation, describes how widespread protests led to a warder at the time saying he would be out in two years. Mandela was hardly forgotten, but until the mid-1970s the apartheid state appeared almost invincible, and this racist arrogance is reflected in the poem 'Rivonia' of 1976, the year in which school children in Soweto punctured that myth. It is ironic that both of the poems in this anthology from that turning point in the country's history were written in Afrikaans, with one of them created not to praise Mandela but to shame him.

In 1980, Oliver Tambo, as president of the ANC, began the "Release Mandela" campaign, focusing on one man as a strategy to put apartheid under the spotlight. The increase in the number of poets from around the world who began to write about Mandela can partly be ascribed to this move, as can the gathering momentum of the anti-apartheid movement around the world and the victory of independence movements in Angola, Mozambique (both 1975) and Zimbabwe (1980).

From the mid-1980s, South Africa came to live under an almost permanent state of emergency and an ever-increasing number of poets began to make the call for Mandela's release part of a much broader democratic struggle to dismantle apartheid and all that it stood for.

By this time Mandela was no longer simply the incarcerated leader of the freedom movement. His status in popular culture had changed from prisoner to icon. He was no longer flesh and blood, or a person who simply required release. He had become a symbol of the suffering that black South Africans endured in the fight for freedom. In one sense it is unusual for so much poetry to have been written about a man who is still alive; such honour is usually saved for martyrs, for those who have sacrificed their lives for the cause of the people. And in many ways he had – but he came out alive. Those writing about him had not given up hope of ever seeing him again, but Mandela the person became increasingly unknowable as his incarceration stretched on, and so he became increasingly more symbol and less flesh and blood.

This is especially the case in those poems written in the upsurge of popular culture inside South Africa from the early 1980s. For this generation the Rivonia trial was part of history rather than memory and Mandela had "never" been a free man. For many of those who took to the streets in 1976, Mandela had been in prison for most of their lives. In many ways he could only exist as symbol, as icon of hope, and that is how his name was used in much poetry. That changed with his release in 1990, and the name of the "living martyr" came to symbolise the possibility that truth and justice can be victorious against the most inhuman of governments.

Many of the poems selected here come from anthologies inspired by the anti-apartheid movement, many of them bearing Mandela's name in the title and celebrating his 70th birthday. These include *MandelAmandla* published in the USA in 1989 and *In the Prison of His Days: For Nelson Mandela* (1988) published in Ireland. From France came *For Nelson Mandela* (1987) with philosopher Jacques Derrida as one of its editors. From Congo (Brazzaville) an anthology published in 1991, *Anthologie Universelle de la Poesie Anti-Apartheid*, came out of a gathering of writers held in Brazzaville in 1987. Almost every poem in this anthology has been previously published, many of them in Anti-Apartheid Movement publications, in tributes to Mandela, in plays, anthologies and on the internet. The poets, mostly South Africans, include a 12-year old boy, musicians, two Nobel laureates, Britain's poet laureate, a former president and, apart from the South Africans, they represent heritages as diverse as Native American, Cuban, Somali, Welsh and Nigerian.

Unsurprisingly, there was an upsurge of poetry in 1990, with Irish Nobel laureate Seamus Heaney adding a section to a play in celebration of this 'rhyming of hope and history'. Just a year earlier another Nobel laureate, Wole Soyinka, had published a collection of poems about Mandela in which he voiced the concerns of many in wondering 'What will be left of you, Mandela?'.

Mandela's humility and conciliatory approach to addressing South Africa's past were not always welcomed, and while there was continued praise for the myth made flesh, there continue to be voices critical of the myth and what that means for the country itself. Examples are the poems by Chris Mann and Tatamkhulu Afrika.

Any mention of Mandela cannot go without a reference to another Mandela whose name was often in the media in the 1980s. Winnie Madikizela-Mandela, Nelson Mandela's former wife, is mentioned side-by-side in some poems from that time. Examples are poems by Nogqaza we Jojo, Kamau Brathwaite, MaryAnn Williams and José Craveirinha. But it is also Craveirinha, in 'Why?', who questions Winnie's controversial suggestion of liberating the country with matches and "necklaces" made from burning tyres.

The process of selecting the poems for this anthology was driven by the desire to allow the story of Mandela, his imprisonment and his accomplishments to be told by poets. The point has been to show how one man on an island evolved from historical event to myth as his incarceration stretched out, and how Mandela, since his release, has combined history and myth in pursuing ideals of humanity. The intention is to present poems as primary historical documents, recording history from an emotional, intimate, subjective perspective.

Despite the tapering-off of poems about Mandela since the flourish of creativity about him at the time of his release in 1990, and the election of a democratic government in 1994, he remains a powerful and unforgettable symbol of justice, of hope, of the power of forgiveness and of reconciliation. He will always be South Africa's, and its inspiration. Unlike most statesmen of his stature, this old man has crept into our hearts – for both political and emotional reasons. This anthology attempts to measure that emotional attachment the world has for South Africa's icon of struggle and of hope.

Richard Bartlett

London, March 2006

On The Island

1

Cement-grey floors and walls
cement-grey days
cement-grey time
and a grey susurration
as of seas breaking
winds blowing
and rains drizzling.

A barred existence
so that one did not need to look
at doors or windows
to know that they were sundered by bars
and one locked in a grey gelid stream
of unmoving time.

2

When the rain came
it came in a quick moving squall
moving across the island
murmuring from afar
then drumming on the roof
then marching fading away.

and sometimes one mistook
the weary tramp of feet
as the men came shuffling from the quarry
white-dust-filmed and shambling
for the rain
that came and drummed and marched away.

3

It was not quite envy
nor impatience
nor irritation
but a mixture of feelings
one felt
for the aloof deep-green dreaming firs
that poised in the island air
withdrawn, composed and still.

4

On Saturday afternoons we were embalmed in time
like specimen moths pressed under glass;
we were immobile in the sunlit afternoon
waiting;
visiting time:
until suddenly like a book snapped shut
all possibilities vanished as zero hour passed
and we knew another week would have to pass.

Rivonia
Air: Viva la 15 Brigata

They have sentenced the men of Rivonia
Rumbala rumbala rumba la
The comrades of Nelson Mandela
Rumbala rumbala rumba la
He is buried alive on an island
Free Mandela Free Mandela
He is buried alive on an island
Free Mandela Free Mandela

Verwoerd feared the mind of Mandela
Rumbala rumbala rumba la
He was stopping the voice of Mandela
Rumbala rumbala rumba la
Free Mbeki Goldberg Sisulu
Free Mandela Free Mandela
Free Mbeki Goldberg Sisulu
Free Mandela Free Mandela

The crime of the men of Rivonia
Rumbala rumbala rumba la
Was to organise farmer and miner
Rumbala rumbala rumba la
Against baasskap and sjambok and kierie
Free Mandela Free Mandela
Against baasskap and sjambok and kierie
Free Mandela Free Mandela

Set free the men of Rivonia
Rumbala rumbala rumba la
Break down the walls of their prison
Rumbala rumbala rumba la
Freedom and justice Uhuru
Free Mandela Free Mandela
Freedom and justice Uhuru
Rumbala rumbala rumba la

Power to the heirs of Luthuli
Rumbala rumbala rumba la
The comrades of Nelson Mandela
Rumbala rumbala rumba la
Spear of the Nation unbroken
Rumbala rumbala rumba la
Amandla Umkhonto we Sizwe
Free Mandela Free Mandela

———

Robben Island

Out there, with little else to do,
A man might spend a year or two
Holding within his splendid view

A mountain mutable, no less
Than the city of changefulness
Crooked in its cradling caress;

For there's a third-degree, a fray
Of time and tide fretting away
From Rocklands round to Grainger Bay;

But slowly, slow as time is to
A man with little else to do
But gaze and gaze on a splendid view.

———

from **Questions and Answers**

After war, after poverty
After war, after poverty
we have become effigies, camera pabulum,
ineffectual scarecrows guarding the corn.
        And the dead point their fingers at some growing girl:
        she shall have tin cans slung from her shoulders,
        she shall have leaden balls on her toes.
We are caught
in colourful postures at shanty entrances
with corrugated faces trapped in Kodacolor.
The Information Bureau do not tell you who
is sweeping Parliament floors after the great
incomprehensible debates of the Potchefstroom Doctors:
the Bloemfontein farmers have more to say
about where I must live and work than
Adam Kok's descendants or Nelson Mandela the lawyer
who because of the golden words that sprang from his black mouth
languishes in a stone cage and may not even
try to swim the Hellespont to Cape Town.

———

*

Yes, Mandela, we shall be moved
We are Men enough to have a conscience
We are men enough to immortalize your song
We are Men enough to look Truth straight in the face

To defy the devils who traded in the human Spirit

For Black cargoes and material superprofits
We emerge to sing a Song of fire with Roland

We emerge to prove Truth cannot be enslaved
In chains or imprisoned in an island inferno
We emerge to stand Truth on her two feet
We emerge

To carry the banner of humanism across the face of the Earth

Our voice in unison with our poet's proudly says
'Change is gonna come!'

———

The Detribalised

He was born in Sophiatown
Or Alexandra, I am not sure,
but certainly not in Soweto.

He skipped school
during playtime
to hock sweets
peanuts, shoelaces,
pilfered in town,
caddied at the golf course.

He can write –
only his name;
He can read –
The World:
"Our one and only paper",
The Golden City Post –
murder, rape and robbery.

He has served time
at the "Fort".
Prison is no shame,
just as unavoidable
and unpleasant
as going to a dentist.

He's a "clever"
not a "moegie";
he never says baas
to no bloody white man.

He wears
the latest Levison's suits
"Made in America";
from Cuthbert's
a pair of Florscheim shoes
"America's finest shoes"
He pays cash
that's why
he's called Mister.

He goes for quality, man,
not quantity, never –
the price is no obstacle.

His furniture is
from Ellis, Bradlow's, exclusive.

Nothing from the O.K. Bazaars
except groceries
and Christmas toys
for their kids.
"Very cheap!" says his wife.

Yes, his wife –
also born in the city, Orlando!
she's pretty,
dresses very well:
costumes from Vanité or Millews.

She's very sophisticated,
uses Artra, Hi-Lite
skin lightening cream,
hair straightened,
wears lipstick
a wig, nail polish:
she can dance
the latest "Monkey"

He married her
after he had fathered
two kids
to prove her fertility.
There's the occasional
domestic quarrel:
he punches her
a "blue eye"
to show her he's the boss.

He takes another cherie
to the movies
at Lyric or Majestic.
They dine at the Kapitan
and sleep at the Planet.

Maybe they go
to a night session
in a posh shebeen:
jazz, booze
knives and guns.

The wife sees
a "nyanga"
to bring her man back home.

He runs a car –
'60 Impala Chev.
Automatic, sleek.

He knows
he must carry a pass.
He don't care for politics
He don't go to church
He knows Sobukwe
He knows Mandela
They're in Robben Island.
"So what? That's not my business!"

―――――

Mandela

You are just number 466/64 to them,
sweeping dusty paths,
tilling and raking the soil of that island.

But you are the strength,
                    the determination
that flows through the veins of your children fighting for you,
                    you and all those numbers.

Yes, with your spade firmly in your hand
                    till and rake the soil Mandela
like your brothers, sisters, sons and daughters
who toil and sweat for Africa.

She is ours
we too shall know no rest
till she comes back to us.

———

And I Watch it in Mandela

It is not to wait until the sky is blue
To turn, look up, and see new light.
The sky has had the colours of violence
For centuries of the agony of the land below it,
And the centuries of truth in the land before it
Bloom only in the flush of new light.

There is fire here;
It is warm,
I am warm,
And I'm comforted.

It has been for this man's life
To paint the new light in the sky.
In all the days when hatred burned
And with its darkness hid the blue,
And in the days to come when black smoke billows still,
This man looks to the deed in the sky.

There is fire here;
It is hot;
I am inflamed,
and I'm heartened.

It is not for the safety of silence
That this man has opened his arms to lead.
The strength of his words hangs in the air
As the strength in his eyes remains on the sky;
And the years of impatient waiting draw on
While this man burns to clear the smoke in the air.

There is fire here,
Which no prison
Can kill in this man;
And I watch it in Mandela.

———

from the Cape to Rio

a great and bitter and dry land...
a land where the earth shudders and jolts
and volcanic mountains have just grown cold...

Table Mountain the prow against which the oceans foam
above the crest the white sails below

because the wind rises
the rigging sings with wind
and like butterflies from an Eastern verse –
but the breakers here are so much higher,
the desert and the wilderness much closer
to the body
there is little refinement
no kings grieving over empires
the only cosmetic the white blind
                    of death –
and yet, like butterflies from a light poem
the yachts shoot out, seeking pleasure beyond the Bay:
the *Old Glory, Jacaranda, Concorde,*
Albatros, Rangoon Lady, Westwind,
Outburst, Impala, Buccaneer, Zwerver,
L'Orgueil, Golden City, Silver Streak
and *Dabulamanzi* –'he-who-cleaves-the-water'

boats and wings and flags sails birds
                    to Rio

past Robben Island

where prisoners can no doubt hear the sails
flap against the sun
where eyes probe so often and so far
into the sun
that like water they can follow
the dots of freedom to the horizon
where they dream that someone anyone
will drain off the water
so that the people can pass dry-shod over False Bay
to the great and promised land
where they dream of the voyage
From Robben Island to the Cape…
brownburnt youngsters set the sails and turn over the breakers
                                there is a pulse and tremor
like the rhythms of a poem
            skirting Robben Island and past, and past
flash *Old Glory, Jacaranda, Concorde…*

ashpale old men bend down
            and count and arrange the grains of salt:

(Translated from Afrikaans by Denis Hirson)

Rivonia

"We know their dream; enough
To know they dreamed and are dead"

Let them be remembered, and what they wanted to do:
let the fear and the blood and violence, death
hatred, vengeance, vandalism and looting, anguish,
pain, agony, noise and racket and rape,
let this, the rejection of order, discipline,
civilisation, love of humanity, let this, I say, never
in all eternity as long as there are those who can think, ever
be forgotten or denied, rather remember;
because dumb-idiotic, presumptuous-impudent are those
who plead for their freedom, would grant them entrance
to the corral of the – granted! – mob,
who would allow them to receive some of that which they wanted to
                    steal,
that is freedom and self-determination, who would again
allow them to walk free to collude with the yellow
and red, who would gently embrace them as brothers
and as friends, who would praise them as tortured heroes
and victims of a Principle, who would then elevate them
to the circle of the blessed – damn crazy!
Because, look, let's mention them by name: Mandela
and Goldberg, Sisulu, Mbeki, Kathrada,
Mhlaba, Mlangeni and Motsoaledi,
with all their helpers and foot-soldiers, and two
that is Goldreich and Wolpe who have disappeared,
and first in rank and deliberation and cunning
Fischer – this band of conspirators (more violently
in opposition to freedom than Kruger was to Milner) and their lackeys
like the murderer Harris or the little boy –
leading-the-sermon, little freedom-struggle warrior Hain,
Let us set aside a chapter for this lot,
then close it, and now together let us
write a history of love and peace that conquers.

(Translated from Afrikaans by Richard Bartlett)

Ever Since My Friend Nelson Mandela
Went to Live on Robben Island

Ever since the court case when my friend Nelson Mandela
sentenced Mr John Vorster to everlasting prison
and decided to live with a few more people
on a tranquil island
it was a shame that 4 million
"whites only" in South Africa
were detained.

And with regard to this, do you know what happened?
Nothing special in psychological terms,
if it were not for the 16 million becoming aware
of their dramatic social dilemma
and posed a political question
which now not even bombs
could turn back.

And after all this, the wife of my friend Nelson Mandela
as her husband had ordered her to leave the domiciliary prison
the freckled Mr. Apartheid ragged with incoherence
towards the end of the afternoon in Winnie's house
will ask: "Dear Nelson
where are we going to go out tonight?"
And my friend Nelson, a kind good-natured husband,
shrugging his shoulders strengthened in the rallies
of solidarity with everyone of the island of solitude
populated by millions in the fortress of ideas
will respond: "I don't know darling."
And unemployed like a worker on holiday
Nelson Mandela will puff out smoke from his pipe
over the ancient route of the Cape of Good Hope,
and with his eyes diving into the Atlantic and the Indian
turning to Winnie will add: "Oh, darling
shall we go to the cinema in Pretoria
or in Soweto?"

And I remember as if it was now the general amnesty,
which my friend Nelson Mandela from the pleasure of his island
                    sojourn
independently of the lion of nerves sharpening his claws on the walls
granted even so to the perpetual condemned Mr. John Vorster
and I also remember the excessive manifestations of gratitude
of the 4 million vaccinated en masse for their fatalistic whiteness
crying out Thank You Very Much when they were exempt
from duties with the vulture Mirages flying over Soweto
with no further taxes to pay for BOSS agents guarding Soweto
and an end to salary deductions to pay for Panhard armoured cars
making Soweto's children nauseous from gunpowder ice-cream
or then everybody free from permanent medical assistance
for contaminated personnel from the uranium laboratories
hidden places of maximum security
manufacturing some ultra-secret thing
that the whole World knows about
except the chief
of a bantustan.

The situation especially regarding
the 4 million South Africans when they were nationalized
into African citizens of the same country as my friend Nelson
                    Mandela
he shooting his name at all the Land's newspapers
from the holiday resort called Robben Island
within the solution on behalf of 16 million people
plus the other 4 million minus BOSS –
because the time factor is vital
for Nelson to go to the cinema
arm in arm with Winnie
be it a theatre in Pretoria
in Johannesburg
or in Soweto.

Regarding the situation of my great friend Nelson Mandela
of the extramarital activity of his wife Winnie
the psychological problems of that old amnestied criminal John
             Vorster
and the phenomenon of Robben Island surrounding South Africa on
             all sides
the measures to be taken are laid bare in this report.

As for the 16 million compatriots of the Mandela couple
working overtime for the benefit of the 4 million
still detained in their respective epidermises
if it wasn't for BOSS
Robben Island
and Soweto
this could be pure demagoguery
but it's a fact!

(Translated from Portuguese by Richard Bartlett)

———

Soweto

For Nelson and Winnie Mandela

Out of this roar of innumerable demons

hot cinema tarzan sweat
rolling moth ball eyes yellow teeth
cries of claws slashes clanks

a faint high pallor

dust

oceans rolling over the dry sand of the savanna

your houses home warm still with the buffalo milk
bladder of elephant tusk of his stripped tree
sing soft clinks

but the barracks

the dark dark barks of the shark
boys
the cool juice of soweto…

■

out of this dust they are coming
our eyes listen out of rhinoceros thunder
darkness of lion

the whale roar stomping in heaven
that black bellied night of hell and helleluia
when all the lights of anger flicker flicker flicker flicker

and we know somewhere there there is real fire
basuto mokhethi namibia azania shaka the zulu kenyatta the shatt
erer the maasai wandering into the everlasting shadow of jah

daughters lost daughters

bellowing against bullhorn and kleghorn
bellowing against bargwart and the searchlights of dogs
bellowing against crick and the kick in the stomach

the acrid wretch against the teeth
bellowing against malan malan malan malan
and boer and boerwreck and boertrek and truckloads of metal

helmet and fusil and the hand grenade
and acid rhodes and the diamonds of oppenheimer
the opulence of voortresshers the grass streiders...

■

suddenly like that fire the crows in johannesburg
you were there
torn.   in tears.   tatters

but the eyes glittered and the fist
clenching around that scream of your mother bled
into a black head of hammers

and the light fell howl
on soweto

the night fell howl
on soweto

and we who had failed to listen all.   those.   foot.   steps
who had given you up like a torn paper package

your heroes   burning in your houses
                    rising from your dust bowls
                    flaring from the sky

                    listen now as the news items lengthen
                    gathering like hawks looking upward like the
                    leopard plunging into the turmoil like the

                    constrictor

and that crouch/shot
shout out against that beast and pistol
the police who shot patrice who castrated kimathi

                    and clattering clattering clattering clattering
                    the veldts gun metals wings
                    rise from their last supper their hunger of bones

                    bomba

and the daniels sing

ukufa akuqheleki kodwa ke
kuthiwa akuhlanga lungehlanga
lalani ngenxeba nikhuzeka

and we are rowing out to sea where the woman
lived with her pipe and her smoke
shack

and her tea in the tea
pot
tankard of hopes

herbs

lamagora afele
izwe lawo

and we are rowing out to sea
where there are farms

and our farmers laid waste the land
to make honey.   we are the bells of the land...

dumminit
dumminit

lit by lantern and lamp

damp
dumminit

ash/can
kero

sene glow
can

dle &
glare

45

dumminit

hitting the head on the h/anvil

huh

drumminit

■

his school/book
huh

but to learn
blood

what is blood
hah

but to bless
dream

and that hill now under the ocean
        and the pages splashed with his blood
        and that bullet a hero a hero herero...

■

once the germans destroyed every sperm
in your village every man who could walk
every nim growing into the noom and nam of his man/hood
they stripped skin and made catapults skulls were their pelmets
upon the wall
and the torn feet cracked and stacked and streggaed

rubbish heap.   dog howl.   cenotaph

and for days there was stench over the grasslands
and for months there was silence upon the trees
cow . goat . udder . manyatta

bantustan upon the land…

and then it was gone like all hero hero herero
like your canoe upon the land…

■

walking back down now from the shores of kikuyu water
washing back down now from swahili laughter

zimbabwe kinshasa limpopo
always limpopo the limper the healer

it comes down from the ruins of the north
from the lakes of the luo

from the sunlights and sunrise of the east

as antient as sheba as wise as the pharaohs
as holy as the early morning mists of ityopia

an i
man
tek long
time to
reach hey
but a
bomb
an de lim
popo drop
down
and de
dread
come
and de
wreck
age soon
done

soon

soon

soweto

we have waited so long for this signal
this howl of your silence
this heat of herero this hero

and i beheld the great beast strangled howling in its chains
led by the fetlocks
and the opulence useless
and the long guns shattered and silent

and we rise

mushroom

mau mau

kilimanjaro

silvers of eagles

tear

savannas

nzingas of rivers

umklaklabulus of mountains

and the unutterable metal of the volcano

rising

rising

rising

burning

soon

soon

soon

soweto

bongo man a come
bongo man a come

bruggadung

bongo man a come
bongo man a come

bruggadung
bruggadung

bruggadung
bruggadung

———

bombs

bombs are something to be scared of they say
in between discussing stock market prices
and terrorists
and now they all lie in bed and sweat
hoping to god that the next one
hurts someone else again
but please lord
please not me

i laugh as i ponder their fear
bombs are not new
they have been going off for some time now
like the big one at sharpeville
like the earthshaker that made them put
mandela away or the one that
caused the special sobukwe clause to be drafted
what about the choerkies
the ones that started to explode
but fizzled out midway
like the crc and the nic
or the ones that failed to detonate
like the homelands
the little toy cocktails
that they handle overseas
and say etcetera…
but i have a bomb
a grey one
that lurks beneath my skull
waiting for the fuse to burn up
from the ink that flows out of my pen
and the nuclear explosion that follows
will spurt out of my ears and mouth
and afterwards we will all ponder
white sensitivity to
black radiation

Robben Island

In a long shot down the rectangular enclosure
stone-walled, with barred windows I find myself
anonymous
among the other faceless prisoners

I see myself again bent on my stone block
crouched over my rockpile
and marvel

I see the men beside me
Peake and Alexander
Mandela and Sisulu
and marvel

All the grim years.
And all the marvellous men
who endure beyond the grim years.
The will to freedom steadily grows
The force, the power, the strength
steadily grows.

———

Mandela

The poem is under my hand.
The images crowd my head.
Poetry is the way
To get this story told.
Poetry has the strength
To tell the story well,
As long as the images hold,
As long as the poem writes.

The Oppressor comes into court.
He is the Prosecutor,
He is the Judge and Jury;
There is no 'win or lose' –
The case is cut and dried.

The Defendant stands alone.
The Prosecutor calls
Himself as Witness – yes,
The Judge upholds the law
That he himself created:
It changes as he chooses.
The Jury only knows
One word – the word is 'Guilty'.

This poem is a gun.
This poem's an assassin.
Images mob my mind...
This pen's a spear, a knife,
A branding-iron, an arrow
Tipped with righteous anger.
It writes with blood and bile.

I take this bitter ink,
Blood-red, to make my mark;
Corruption from the wound,
Sap from the poison-tree,
Aloe and gall and myrrh.

This poem's a loaded gun,
This verse a Kalashnikov.
I aim it at the snake
That slithers to our children
And strikes! See where the tell-tale
Blood-beads pearl on the skin.
The snake, the Prosecutor,
The Oppressor, the Judge, the Jury –
You must always aim for the head.

This poem is a gun
And words are ammunition.

This poem tells a story
That can't be cut or censored.

This poem's not up for sale,
It can't be bought as men
And cattle can be bought,
So don't make me an offer,
Put your money back
In your purse… But you can listen,
Everyone can listen,
Not just the great and good,
Not just Nelson Mandela.

Judge and Jury, listen!
Prosecutor, listen!
Policeman, come and listen!
Turnkey, come and listen!
You who perjure, listen!
You who torture, listen!
I want you to hear this poem;
I want you to hear me speak
As if I were Mandela.
I speak for him – Mandela.
I speak for an angry man,
A man whose voice was stopped,
A man whose mouth was gagged
Because he once said, 'No!'
'No!' to the Prosecutor,
'No!' to the Judge and Jury,
'No!' to injustice, 'No!'
To indignity and oppression.

He says, 'Don't think I'm beaten;
Don't think of me as weak
Or wretched. I'm no slave.
I'm not destitute
Although they stole from me.
I'm not without a home
Although my land's been taken.
Don't pity me; don't tell me
I'll have my chance at glory.

Didn't Jesus ask us
To turn the other cheek
And give the Fool who slaps us
Another chance to show us
Just how much he hates us?
And if that Fool should kill me:
Tell me, who's the victor?

He thinks of me, that man,
As someone who has no-one:
No friends, no family,
No allies, no supporters.
He cannot see the circle –
Right round the globe – of people,
All races, colours, creeds,
Calling out for justice.
If I say I'm hungry
I mean hungry for justice.
If I say I'm hog-tied
I mean hog-tied by lies.
If I say I'm blind,
I'm blind to compromise.

If I say an angel
Stands at my right shoulder
I mean 'Angel of Death',
I mean 'Death in Disguise'.

Everything I've suffered,
Everything I've dreamed of,
Are mine and mine alone.

The Judge and Jury know me.
They know what I have suffered.
They think that what I'm thinking
Is what they think I'm thinking.
It's not. If I say 'Angel'
I mean Angel of Death.
I mean the Angel's shadow
That darkens all my thinking.

The brush they use to sweep
My thoughts out of the door
Is worn down to the shaft.
Only the thoughts are left.

The snake-bite and the blood-beads,
The blood-beads and the poison,
Are my immunity.

Once my sleep was dreamless,
Once my mind was blank;
Now my dreams are rich,
My every thought is clear.

Now I see a way –
A way others have taken;
It's called the Road to Freedom.'

I want you to hear him speak:
Hear Mandela's wisdom.
Listen, all who hear me,
All who think as I do.
Abu Hadra – hear me!
Poet and friend, now listen!
I know you'll understand.

This poem's a ransom-note,
Blood-money to the many
Who cry aloud for justice.
It's payback to Mandela
And everything he stands for
And everyone he speaks for.

This poem has a blade
Hidden at its heart.
That steel will last forever!

So listen, Abu Hadra!
If you will listen, others
Will listen too, will hear
The words as if Mandela
Was calling them to arms.
They'll grasp the blade that's hidden
Deep inside this poem;
They'll show the Judge and Jury
The cutting-edge of freedom;
They'll show the Prosecutor
The blade that lasts forever;
They'll never bow their heads
Or walk in chains and fetters.

This poem is a mirror
I've made for us, Hadraawi,
A mirror we can hold up
To show the ignoramus
The depth of self-deception
That lies in his reflection;
To show the Judge and Jury
How the wide world sees them;
To show the man who takes
Pleasure in pain the guern
Of glee that warps his smile.

Hadraawi, read this poem
To anyone who'll listen.
Help them to find the voice
I've given to Mandela.
And tell them this: our purpose
Is peace; our password 'Freedom';
Our aim, equality;
Our way, the way of light.

(Literal translation from Somali by Martin Orwin and Maxamed Xasan 'Alto'.
English version by David Harsent)

58

Echo of Mandela

In silence
the distant heroes bow their
heads
the chains weigh them down
they know no laughter
retreating ... retreating
into a mist of bloodiness
the decaying skull
of buried freedom
emits a dull echo
of cries
free me
free me
the people are calling
looking back
they see nothing but death
where is the welcome
why the sound of tears
hammering ... hammering
those coffins of confessions
the decaying skull
of buried freedom
emits a dull echo
of cries
free me
free me
the people are calling
tomorrow has come
the distant heroes stand above
they look down
they shake their heads
whispering ... whispering
into ears of emptiness
the decaying skull
of buried freedom
emits a dull echo

of cries
free me
free me
the people are calling
South Africa, are you listening?

―――

Please Keep Your Children Under Control

On the cast-iron assegaai-emblazoned gates of the Voortrekker
        Monument the following words boast:

'WHITES ONLY

NO ADULTS WITHOUT SHOES
NO WOMEN WEARING TIGHT SHORTS
NO MEN WEARING SHIRTS WITHOUT COLLARS OR
        SLEEVES

PLEASE KEEP YOUR CHILDREN UNDER CONTROL
                                    BY ORDER'

'KEEP YOUR CHILDREN UNDER CONTROL!'
Tell them about Piet Retief
Dingaan's betrayal
Umgungundlovu and Bloukrans
the blood, blood…
Blood River!

Remember

Paul Kruger
D.F. Malan
Hendrik Verwoerd
P.W. Botha

we bled in struggle
but it has become scab in monument and sculpture
we have overcome
because it is rulers' blood that flows in us

little Dinky-Toy child in the park
little protected child in the house
little warm child in the winter
happy little one in the suburb

madam child
boss child!
Pretoria child!

little bright blue-eyed child
hop, skip and a jump
'In South Africa our land!'

'KEEP YOUR CHILDREN UNDER CONTROL!'

Tell them about Piet Retief
Dingaan's betrayal
Umgungundlovu and Bloukrans
the blood, the blood…
Blood River

Forget
Chaka
Oliver Tambo
Steve Biko
Nelson Mandela

we bled in struggle
but it has become scab in monument and sculpture
we have overcome you
because it is ruler's blood that flows in us

little wire-car child
from the dusty streets
little hungry-child of the empty pots
little barefoot-child of the frost
scared little child of the township

wash-maid child
kaffir child!
Soweto child!

> little muddy brown-eyed child
> hop, skip and a jump
> 'Umkhonto we Sizwe i'Afrika!'

(Translated from Afrikaans by Richard Bartlett)

———

robben island my cross my house

morning
cape town
harbour
picture
handcuff
manacle
chains

between chain
and chain
our fence posts
the iron
of imprisonment
rattles
on the bellwethers

mute sea
shivers
from gleaming

a ferry awaits
nodding
for its ten terrorists

we laugh
at the iron façade
the deathly cold-sweat fear
of their heart

on the quay
the black workers
laugh
with us

this way
that way
watershed
between hell
greater hell
what does it matter
because who
doesn't know
of robben island
and its zealous
masters
the anxious
green helicopter
on our head

then we sink
chain-bound
bait
below decks
of the boat
and the workers
don't greet us

porthole
o porthole
tell table mountain
we say hello and goodbye

island
by midday you
already
have a wet
noose
around your neck
your tongue swells up
from the sea
a hunchback

you die

because you must die
ten terrorists
watch your approach
through all your barbed wire
your granite jail
grinds its steel teeth

but you have leprosy
unwillingly
admitted
you must literally
fall apart
we are your backbone
and your death

you die

i get hungry
the metal bowls
row upon row
like open hands
then comes order
chicken mealies
feed
on its poultry

i peck peck
but my dumb mouth
seeks food
mealies slip
sideways
out on to the cement floor
until i am fed up
learning
your art

and to quench
my thirst
i drink noisily
water
from your fonta mara

the night also comes
i wonder
about the moon
on your cell's
iron fingers
i pull myself up
i see moonlight
on your stone slate
the moon has gone
the star
the universe
i hang
black silhouette
on the bars
of your blindfold

but i phoenix
jump up
out of my unbending flesh
see there
the moon
the star
the milky way
macros
out of micros

how can concrete
steel
crucify

i transcend
i moon
i sun
i milky way
i cosmos
i laugh
at your jack-boot
at your futility

because i was led
from your house of slavery
i stagger away
from promised lands
led
from houses of slavery
this land
is our land

yesterday
robben island
i see your face
close ups
of devil's peak
of blouberg strand
must you zoomlens
must you look-on

at long distances
there are here
no prisoners
the h-blocks
the kulukuthu
the lonely confinement
the single cells
of the makulu team
stand empty

freedom fighter-foreigner
on blouberg strand
on the devil's peaks
you do not peck at night
chicken feed
can't know
of the yellow grass mat
on the indifferent floor

at night
the wind blows
around the world's
prison corners

then the guard-dog barks
scared
and the warders
swear f.n.-ly
in their sleep

yesterday
robben island was
here in front of me
hunted
like a scavenger
frightened and growling
i become chill
dead still
for the strange thing
that waits

but from devil's peak
at night flickers
the lighthouse
and nobody feels
the bellow
of the foghorn

blouberg beaches
you will always
look at me
but even now you don't know
how the wood camp
is enclosed
with barbed wire

sea point
your streets
your beach
whoring
next to the slate quarry
but the boil
you do not see harden
to callous

table mountain
you look down
on the white oven
of the lime quarry
how many picks
swinging
do you see the skull
split

yesterday
robben island
had been here with me
blackandwhite
scared

we arrive
terrorist section
a welcoming
breaks
open like a new era
the new namibia
spills over the camp
warm
like a brazier
from childhood
and next to the barbed wire
is a torchbearer
obstinate
at the
crucible
of the oshakati
smallholder
and the golden
proletariat
the hatred
the jack-boot
and the barbed wire

then tears
the veil
of robben island
the earth shakes
twilight settles
i wake up
reborn

the black light
is white seagulls
thousands
and i watch anxiously
for the coming
collision
but they cross
triumphantly
free

the first morning
the brass bell
clangs me awake
disoriented
my child
earthquake
out to safety
i run
i stumble
i fall
over the feet
of ten terrorists

outside

i hear
how the gravel
on his teeth
grinds
jack-boots
my god
robben island

i must get up
i must salt-water shower
sticky
cold
fascist

the old men
standing grey-grey
shivering

just like
machine guns
also shiver

we stand to attention
before the chosen few
red cards
in front of the chest
grotesque
ritual

then the sun grows
out of the skin
of the sea
a yellow boil
of a day

the barbed wire
glistens
it dews
on robben island
too

a jack-boot
talks
wood camp get moving
wood camp get moving
closer to the wood camp as
the dog hangs
on its leash

it is a nice day
the feet protest
on the shell gravel
it sounds nice
we twitter
like autumn birds

the silent warders
hang
on their dogs
and an f.n.
is cold
in the winter
the winter
winter

it is a nice day

i smell the sea
astonished
at the dead structures
of world war
over democracy

the warders' shining
shoes
are faded
the dogs
are flapping tongues
the f.n.
still cold

it is a nice day

the seagulls
at the breeding colony
burst out loudly
open
like pamphlet bombs
i read their
hesitant
political writings

the warders
look up alarmed
the dogs
duck
in their leashes
caught
an f.n. falls
nearly

it is a nice day

the wood camp
is here

i see the rope
of barbed wire
one by one
i slip
into its thorny covering
terrorist
with shining axe
chops
woodchips fly
in slave land
sawing through
the rooikrans wood

because tonight
the little people are making
fire
tonight
the little people are making
fire

my beloved
hangs on a barbed wire
my beloved
hangs on a barbed wire
my beloved
hangs on a thorny-bush
wire

it is a nice day

the warders
are a covering
cordon
it's natural
they look
f.n.-ly
at terrorist
but in the wood pile
forever lies
a bag of newspapers

it is a nice day

especially
i comrade
pendulate
boer's tub
in the sea
we wipe his shit
off with newspaper
until insulation
disappears

f.n. watch
us suspiciously
but the shell gravel
already grinds
to the cells

the night
smallholder sits
city worker sits
intellectual sits
the do-not commands
of the island
being read

and in the dark
at wood camp
at lime quarry
at slate quarry
the seagulls hold
mass protests

in h-cells
through the night
meanings slam
into pieces
against a rock
of antithesis

but tomorrow
dripped water
flows
back to a sea
of petition

brass bell rings
again
jack-boots gnash
intimidate
watch

for the red card
for the attention
before god
of god
of tom, dick and harry

but look
in my right hand
is the whitepaper
of revolution two
in revolution one

then the herrenvolk
wriggles
in my hand
like a snake
poisonous

the kulukuthu
falls open
the red sea
of isolated
imprisonment

then splashes
the water
becomes quiet
around my engorged
heartbeat

it is dark
on robben island
the hours
lie quietly
like swamp water

my child's head
swells at night
out of the stinking
porridgeness
a gas bubble

an animal
peers
through its iron fingers
at the cocoon
of a quiet person

i hear a giggle
i weep
a tear
i fade
i disillusion
sometimes
i become openly
weak
bloody tired
i want to go home
i get tired

from all day jail
drunk
banging about
in the spaces
of existential
freedom

saturday nights
rubbed in
the absurdity
of a spaceless
loneliness

i sink
away
in wakeful dream
in rosekrans
that i gingerly
feel
its seven
stations
of suffering
i am namelessly
lonely

my daughter
waits
at the window
i disappear
like a good dream
she struggles
every day
to cry
me back
but i am her lonely
imprisonment

i long
for my wife
i become tactile
poor
i yearn
for someone
in my intimate
space
i am cold
lonely
like a jail cell

luckhoff street
bloody far off town
i play dassiebol
in a location
of cirasvlei

i put my hard toes
in bra cecil's
fresh shit
hell
cecil
can't you shit
somewhere else
bloody far away

i slam the lid
of a tin closed
with a stone
tin-i-spy's
summer night

i wait
again for daddy
scared
the wood is wet
i throw lampoil
on a lame
flame
but the fire
doesn't want to burn
tonight
i again get
pissed off

i play aamblou
i shriek with joy
past the manacles
and the washing water channels
on the street sand

but every day
my dream is
a slit
i see an iron
penis
ramrod stiff
like an erection
in the vagina
of my cell
my freedom
shrugged off
shot in the snatch
caught up

i am wasted
i lie cold
and slimy
on the sement floor
spilt out

now at night i lick
my food
a dog
a mongrel
shudders over my snout
my claw
turns black
a beggar
a stench

now i no
longer fly
as before
i hijack
every boeing
d.f.-malan
very high
over havana
i build a revolution
i am god
of proletariat
of smallholder
i fantasize
powerful dams
in the great karoo
i see hunger
evaporate
the millennium
arriving
but now
i am fallen flat
like a failed
plan

until a new day
breaks open
a fresh orange
juicy

single cells
makulu team
how much mythology
do i still discover
in the re-revolt
but now
i am jubilation
i am joy
i am powerful
like revolution

icarus
i cleanse
in the sun
brotherhood
becomes clear
in the searchlight

brothers
fall back
to earth
in the love nest
of struggle

oh robben island
my cross
my house
i recover
from lonely
imprisonment
i don't
feel the horror
of the grass mat
i still smell
the piercing
stench
of the tub
i hold
my hungry hands
over the warm flame
of the human voice

i make by b.b. pill
i smoke
everything is a yellow glow
and nearby
everything is human
a cosy blanket
around my tired
spirit
i sleep –

the high
lightbulb
glimmers
a southeaster
blows
tomorrow it will rain

the day arrives again
brass bell
metal master
march
energetically
down the corridor
the single cells
explode
with communist
threats
total onslaught
freedom fighter
your slop-bucket
hangs desperately
on my crooked
fingers

you eat today
boss's braaipap
without braai
it's nice
because around me sit
makulu team
i pull the bars
around me tightly
safe

i am in the valley
of the shadow of death
i fear
no evil
because you are with me
makulu team

three-three
to the beach

because by the sweat
of my brow
will you earn
your bread
herrenvolk

do you see i pull
the fresh seaweed
wet
tough
stuck in the knotted root
of the ideology

we become entwined
makulu team

the sun burns
reality
around itself
a seaweed shoot
sometimes leaves
the compost
i stumble
after my battle
i am dead tired

makulu team

i hurry
myself to my cell
but the music
of makulu team
blares
after me
cosy
imprisonment

i shower
in the crucible
struggle honed
struggle honed
on the edge
of woolly haired gorge
proletariat
you want to be mist
smallholder
you want to be mist
i shrink
from the clinging
pain

below me
the high flame
burns
of chosen ones
cosy
continuing

the cool rain
is gone
the day is dry
and switched on

in the lime quarry
herrenvolk bury
marxisms
i peck
scratches
in the hard white lime
i thesis
i antithesis
a bloody great
dialectic
showers struggling
over the quarry
a lorry awaits

but at night
i drag my pick
and spade
to the toolbox
sober

under the white lime
deep
lies marx
fossilised

and f.n.
watches sneering
over the big amphitheatre
of the quarry
at the varnished
undertakers

at night
i stumble back
freudian-like
in my placental
cell
bourgeois
study books
i relax
in the psychedelic
reality
of capital
every time
infantile
i kick
the abdominal wall
of robben island

drugged
i listen
to the far-off bark
of the guard-dog
the watch towers
dim
a foghorn
clamors in vain
i drift
away
to a pleasant freedom
on the rocks
the sea
sparkles
at blouberg strand
my child maintains
fold over me
powerful arms
peaceful
i step
on the sponge
of winter grass
in my mother-fucking
backyard
daddy
has my hand
on the hills
of helshoogte
we rush
along the slopes
down

i laugh
the school bell
rings
i run
on the playground
i cannot
be late
the brass bell
rings
it gnashes
i know
the sound

i hear the freedom-fighter
in the corridor
every morning
i am born

today i must
break the bluestone
i walk quietly
next to the myths
of a twisted
revolution
makulu team
today i will
break the bluestone
i walk quietly
along the coast
the cannon
watches desolate
over the sea
today
i break the bluestone
i walk quietly
the wooden camp
lies splintered
between barbed wire
the sea jumps
up against the rocks
to see
who steals newspapers
in the grease pit
the old men
break columns
to water
they burst out
laughing

i walk quietly
to the bluestone quarry
seagulls everywhere
like a struggle
won
i carry my hammer
in a right-hand
down in a quarry
where the water
is quiet like a stone
i start to break
proletariat
smallholder
i must hit bloody hard to free you
from the stone
but the stone
is hard
i smell the sulphur
from the blow

the sun sets
like a boil
in the cool sea

tomorrow
you and i again
hit
the stone atom
must split

we walk to the cell
alongside years
the cannon flakes
new tubs
blossom in the flower garden
the bars grow
lusciously
from the stone wall
sometimes
we catch birds
in clever snares
from the gallows
or pluck
mussels
next to the sea

christmas swings
the road
towards new year
six times
the brass bell
sobs
for auld lang syne
but the quarry
remains harsh

at the harbour
the visitors' halls
wait
contrite
the wood camp
dies
o lime quarry
you are the shallow
grave
you must open
like a resurrection
we desecrate
your constant

the stone quarry
becomes quiet
the stone cracks
the workers
shake
their picks
the shining
seaweed
breaks more easily
now

the foghorn
bellows still
lost nightly
the guard-dogs
bark
at the full moon
of the cape
the sea
bashes
its head
broken
against the jail
walls

the f.n.'s
mouth
drags in the dust
the guards
look gloomy
like winter rains

on the island harbour
the ferry waits
nodding
at ten terrorists
who are going
home

(Translated from Afrikaans by Richard Bartlett)

The ABC Jig

Anger comes in silence

Some of our brothers graduate
on Robben Island
in the Arts of Struggle;
Others graduate
on the plains of the African Savannah;
Others still,
in the malaria-infested bushes
of the Boerewors Curtain.

Yet anger grows in silence

When they took us in
Steve Biko had resurrected
Onkgopotse, Mdluli, Mapetla;
I had seen them
give breath unto the clay
of our liberated Black manchild.

Black is alive & keeping

The S.B.s swarmed over us
leaving their stings of State fear
in our Black-Star shoulders;
You'd swear
it was the Gestapo squads
on Jew hunts.

The hunter shall be the hunted

They tortured our Black souls
little knowing:
By detaining us
            they had sent us on a Black Holiday:
By assaulting us
            they were teaching us hate;
By insulting us:
            they were telling us never
            to turn the other cheek.
We have no more tears to shed.

            Ours is the long stride

It A Come

It a come
fire a go bun
blood a go run
No care how yuh teck it
some haffi regret it

Yuh coulda vex till yuh blue
I a reveal it to you
dat cut-eye cut-eye cyaan
cut dis-ya reality in two

It a come
fire a go bun
blood a go run
it goin go teck you
it goin go teck you

so Maggie Thatcher
yuh better watch ya
yuh goin go meet yuh Waterloo
yuh can stay deh a screw
I a subpoena you
from de little fella
call Nelson Mandela
who goin tun a martyr
fi yuh stop support
de blood-suckin I
call apartheid

for it a come
blood a go run
it goin go teck you
it goin go teck you

an if yuh inna yuh mansion
a get some passion
it goin go bus out in deh
like a fusion bomb
it a swell up inna de groun
an yuh cyaan hold it back
yuh haffi subscribe to it
or feel it

an no bodder run to no politician
for im cyaan bribe dis-ya one
an no bodder teck it fi joke
yuh no see wha happen to de Pope

It a come
fire a go bun
blood a go run
it goin go teck you
it goin go teck you
Some goin go call it awareness
an we goin go celebrate it wid firmness
Odders goin go call it revolution
but I prefer liberation

Fi de oppressed an de dispossessed
who has been restless
a full time dem get some rest

for it a come
fire a go bun
blood a go run
it going go teck you
it going go teck you

not only fi I
but fi you too

Death Row

I

The first we hear is this tremendous
                    cajoling laughter.

ten minutes later, above our cells
Squeak-squeak-squeak, across the catwalk
Walks an unfamiliar warder.

It's three fokken terrorists – he says,
Not grasping, yet,

Who we are.
They're impossible, man. A person
Can't do
Nothing with them.

Johannes Shabangu.
David Moise.
Bobby Tsotsobe.

Having
Skipped the country
        trained in diverse parts
                slipped in clandestinely

Dug   diggers of earth
                residers of holes underground.
Sons of the soil
        breath to be swallowed
                breath swallowed by the night
In the night
        darker than plain dark
                and all so quiet
Sappers
        Soweto's sons
                stalkers
                        Who blew up
Sasol 2 by Secunda
        Uncle Tom's Hall
                Booysens, the cop shop
Dube line
        likewise a place
                near Malelane
                        Caught
Caught in a shoot-out
        captured at Matola
                strung upside down
Probed without days
        in a night
                in a river of needles
The clammy hood
        choke hold
                a year without season
For months
your bodies probed
                months long until

finally you were led
unbowed into court
and charged
all three
with high treason.

Now nine months already, brothers
You've been sitting
On death row.

II

What concerning C section
can I tell you?

What down here could be different
from B section?
A section? Or from wherever
it is inside this slaughter house
they've just randomly shifted you from?

Listen…two walls to the left.
A garden – I think,
from where this sound
leaks in.
A guinea-hen's call – we've been told,
glass on glass
a pocketful of marbles weeping
deep in her throat, but don't ask

On Wednesday mornings
almost every other week,
another, a staggered sound
like bioscope seats flapped
back, What's that!? Don't

Ask me, brothers, I

…Perhaps I didn't hear.

III

Of course we never get to speak,
As such, to each other.
We're still fifty yards, one corridor,
Many locked locks apart.

Nkosi sikelele', we try singing, at night.
Us down here, to you,
Three condemneds, along there.

Morena...we whiteys sing,
Mayibuye iAfrika, and muffled
far-off chortling, you guys
Call back: *Encore! Encore!*

IV

Then it's you singing slow
Antiphonal phrases,
Three tongues floating over
                    That audible
Drop which gathers,
The words thrumming in your
Throats, brothers,
                    About which
Some Wednesday morning
                    Three nooses will go.

                    One voice leading:
Arrraaise ye, high up,
Every night,
                    Deeper, two in the chorus:
Prisoners from your slumbers
Called and
                    To boil or
Respond like a
Ripple like a
Lurch like a
                    Ukuhlabelela
is to
                    Glow like a

Growl like a
   Glow like a
Boil like a
   Bean stew like a
Ripple like a
Bus queue weaves like a
Moves like a
   Stalks like a
Moves like a
Fighter
Ukuhlabelela
   Three voices
Called or
   Moise
Combine or responding
   Tsotsobe
Weaving
Shabangu
In and
   Voices
Each other
   Around of, sliding
Into each night's
Finale, all three
Three now
As one: *Tha-a-a*
Inta
nasha – na – ale
yoonites tha
hooman
reiss, a-MAA
   - ndla! longleev
sisulu-mandela-tambo
LONGleev! LONGleev!
   shouted *longleev!*
Your voices, brothers
Down these concrete
Corridors of power.

A song for Mandela

Inside of me
> In this blackened casket
> wounds lie sealed like bodies in vault;
> shouts of anger crackle like flames
> in the fireplace of injustice

Beneath me
> impatient tremors burst out
> to break the dry olive branch of peace
> sold at the marketplace of deception

Around me
> the precious womb that bled me to life;
> flesh that clothed my soul
> and gave it wings...
> > Yet even a mother's love
> > Is fragile to torment and to terror

Beside me
> heavy footfalls of running men
> cries of thwarted souls rush like restless rain
> from the skies of despair

Near me
> I hear the staunch march of anxious feet
> carrying the sounds of defiance
> > Not alone, God not alone
> > Will we rise up to repossess our land
> > Truth is witness to our wrath
> > and our commitment
> > Evil has had its day...

Beside me
> Around and beneath me;
> Inside this burning self
> Where impatient drums
> Beat a martial song
> I hear Mandela singing:
> > Unzima lomtwalo
> > Ufuna amadoda...

———

Nothing New in the South

To teacher Craveirinha

There further to the South
Mandela
continues to dream of a star
Soweto's electric guitars
vomit notes of blood
over the skies of Johannesburg
while Miriam Makeba
suffers exile in Guinea
There are youths dying
committing suicide Smandje-Mandje
in a black and white contrast
with a multinational sumptuousness
in the brothels of Transkei
Mama Winnie
that coherent pregnancy
continues to dream of an intimate gesture from Nelson
after centuries of separation
how is play possible
in-between Vorster and Botha
between her and the kisses of her hero
On Robben
there is a non-racist militant who is dying
and the survivors chant Nkosi Sikelele
while the night of Southern Africa
gains another star
which is not yet
the star with which Mandela dreams
I have heard it said
in newspapers and on the radio
that the children of Gandhi and others disinherited
are gaining the right to vote there in the South
Just that the warriors of Chaka
are being shot dead or hanged
in an organised and efficient rehearsal
of a new modern edition
of Dingaan's Day

(Translated from Portuguese by Richard Bartlett)

Mister Mandela

Forgive me Mister Mandela
I tried to picture you in prison
for twenty-five years
but a hand closed on my throat

I know this land
It lives in the windowless room
of my childhood
A room filled with rats and menacing sounds

A terrifying loneliness
Seizes my insides
closes my voice
and I don't want to remember

In the dark, eyes shut tight
the memories of an empty belly
force themselves to fill the space
where thought of you ought to live

The sight of your Black face
between stark white walls and iron bars
draws the drapes on the ray of light
left me by a thousand rain-soaked days

When I look at you in prison, Mr. Mandela
I can't feel the power of mother sea
feel the wind off my green mountains
or rise up to resist their demise

I treasure this eagle of resistance
couching you and Leonard in each wing
you shall have to be happy, Mr. Mandela
with my humble tribute

———

Nelson Mandela

I will learn in your name
a lesson of courage
and I will compose in your honour
a new hymn.

From now on,
I will learn in your name
a lesson of dignity
and the face of Africa in struggle.

(Translated from Portuguese by Richard Bartlett)

———

Mandela

This name is a signal
saintly and secret
of a clandestine present
a shining light
guiding the future

This name
over Commissioner Street
in the small hours
silences the neon lights of Hillbrow
darkens the corridors of parliament
multiplies in telexes
but rests always in the townships
in the hearts of the townships.

This name flies in the rock
Between the hand and the police Casspir
forming an arc of freedom.

(Translated from Portuguese by Richard Bartlett)

Soweto

They are witnesses
To the sadistic law,
The adamant blacks
Huddling together outside their round huts
To celebrate death again
Under an Afrikaner.
From their hands come rhythms of belief
In the future of the ebony race;
In their voices, the burning key
To generations of service –

Viva Mandela! Viva Sisulu!
Viva Tambo and Desmond Tutu!

They come in their twilight dance
To the edges of their narrow world,
Here in the graveyard of Soweto's hill
Accompanied by the clatter of a helicopter
And the threat of Botha's barrels
To kneel as usual
Before the coffins of their sacrifice.
In their tempestuous grief
You can hear the ring of their chains
Whipping the sun –

Viva Mandela! Viva Sisulu!
Viva Tambo and Desmond Tutu!

Then come the white hounds
Triumphant with their guns,
To surround them noisily,
And the chill of Golgotha
Is in their bullet threat;
Interrupting the sad ballet,
Death spreads out from their tanks
And raises a revolution from the sweat
Of their earnest devotion.
The passion of the black enclosed place will cluster
And blood will come again from the desecration,
But the Boer's fist
Will not quench the black creed
Or its just clamour.

Viva Mandela! Viva Sisulu!
Viva Tambo and Desmond Tutu!

(Translated from Welsh by Ann Reckless)

———

Hero of Heroes

Another dead body in the streets,
            "Imigqakhwana Yeetishala"
            – Bastards –
I cursed
as I struggled through the printed word.
They've turned this land
into a graveyard
where one day there won't be
marble enough
to honour all these youngsters
cut down so cruelly
in their prime;
            "Iqhawe Lama Qhawe"
            – Hero of Heroes –
who left no offspring
to swell the ranks
of the ancestral gods;
            "Iqhawe Lama Qhawe"
Monuments of Marble
in the South…..

———

Well, good morning...

'Well, good morning, how are you'
Every Thursday morning, 'Ha ha!'
It's the same old thing without fail,
'I'm remarkably well!'

'Well, how are things in Johannesburg?
I'm remarkably well here.'
'My God, I'm hearing Welsh – excuse me – belch.
What's Welsh for mine's a gin?'

'Ha ha, yes yes, rugby rugby.
If I remember rightly
We met in '73
Near the Loftus Versveld Ground.'

'Yes, Alun, I remember the evening,
Fine singing – good singing –
Calon Lan and Gwlad y Gan
Yes yes, rugby rugby, ha ha.

'Half the Lions were there
As well, of course, as yourself,
and the nice little blacks in dickie bows
serving the G and T.

'I feel completely at home here
The country is first rate
The sea is blue, the veld so vast
Attitudes so out of date.'

'Is that so! But what about politics,
Don't those blacks give any trouble?'
'No problems, Al, they're easy to get
To work in your house.'

Thursday morning between sleep and waking,
While listening to this nonsense,
A small voice came across the line:
'Free Nelson Mandela!'

(Translated from Welsh by Ann Reckless)

———

Madiba
(17 June 1986, Meyerton Police Station)

They tried with all their laws
And jail doors
To keep you away from us.
but they failed.

From our cradles you
were made beast,
A man of all evil,
An immoral man,
A man to be scorned and scoffed.
A man unfit to live and lead.

So many times they lied, tried and failed.
Your words of wisdom,
continue to inspire and show
Us the way.

From behind the heavy jail doors,
Through thick prison walls,
We hear your voice, loud and clear,
Unbowed and unblunted
By decades of confinement and degradation:
"I shall start where I left off!"
Just yesterday you coughed:
"All power to the people!"
Delighting our hearts and gushing
Wintry winds into the corridors of power.

Your name today is haloed,
Round the world streets bear your name,
Sculptors and painters grace
Places with your face.
From lips of babes we hear:
"uMandela ubabawethu!..."

The M-Plan showers our streets with People's Power,
The rulers are confused about you:
To release or not to release you is the question.
Things falling
Apartheid centre can no longer hold.

The masses demand your freedom,
Even more: they march to free you.
"I shall return!"
"I must return!" you vowed.

———

To Nelson Mandela

Guardian of my dignity
I was not a free man
Until you set me free

You make me BE
Black
Under real conditions
Protecting my freedom always
Moulded in your image
Those of us who cannot
Turn away from our identity
Who have only the strength
Of our honour.

I have to die
Black
For that is my identity.

In your image
Soul Brother.

(Translated from French by Michael Dewar)

_____

Like a Field of Love

No road leads to where he lives
everything is under siege – the streets a graveyard
but far away, above his house,
a roving moon
grasped
in strands of dust.

Let him keep his secrets
now he sets the sea in his guts
now he sets it at his window
let him keep his secrets
disguise himself as a bud
clothe the face with a stone
let him keep his secrets
like a field of love
that each season metamorphoses
and leafs the trees

He knows the birds
that perch on their voices
and fly with branches

The farthest light
is nearer than the nearest dark
distance
a myth
probably

The massacre changed the image of the town
this stone
a child's head
this smoke
men's breath

Birds refuse to sing
in fields where silence is unknown

———

You Whom I Call!...

You whom I love without ever having met
You to whom nobody talks anymore
You in whom lives the lonely music
You who took the name of silence
You who took the veil of the night
You a man of all time
You a man of all ages
I hold you most dear in the depths of my memory
From deep within comes my love of the homeland
And the echo of your voice
Oh you, nelson MANDELA!
Oh you whom I call Lumumba!
Oh you whom I call Che Guevara!
Oh you whom I call Kwame Nkrumah!
Oh you whom I call Salvador Allende!
Oh you whom I call Hoji Ya Hende!
Oh you ... whom I call the son of the people
Leading a band of your race
Towards the noble mission of humanity
Taking into your heart all greatness
All evidence of every violated race.

(Translated from French by Michael Dewar)

———

The Burnt Hut

(To Benjamin MOLOISE, to Nelson MANDELA)

Yes! She burned
She burned from a bolt of lightning
A bolt of lightening that struck the hut
The hut of my father
And the hut burned
We were left without shelter, without a home
And I cried.

Yes! She fell
Surprised by death
She fell
Dead on the path that led to the spring
My grandmother fell in action
We were left without her, without a grandmother
And I cried.

Yes! It came
Alarming and surprising news
Since, a poet came and went
Shot down one fine day
Benjamin Moloise passed away in action
We were left without Benjamin, without a poet
And I cried.

Yes! they arrested him
Arrested and thrown into prison
Nelson Mandela was arrested
They arrested and threw him in prison over two decades ago
The white minority in power arrested him
And here we are without Mandela, without a leader
And I continue to cry.

(Translated from French by Michael Dewar)

119

Why?

A troubled sky bereft of clouds
spreads over the location
and hangs over the cities.

But ...

why gross Firestone neckbands
why the rank smell of GoodYear collars
to add a final touch
to the ceremonious attire
of robot men
set on fire?

I know that my friend Nelson
is just as averse as I am
to the pyrotechnics
of that pungent smell
of an after-shave of burning rubber
melting the closely shaved neck
for once and for all
into black pitch.

Why

my sister Winnie?

My sister Winnie Mandela
why?

(Translated from the Portuguese by Luis Mitras)

———

Canto Three
(from **The Civil War Cantos**)

Ghosts you, escaped from the corpses' acre,
blood congealed on your brow –
one hole through your brain –
you walk through the smoking ruins of our Civil Wars:
undefeated. Born
in the years of silence you waited your time:
unfolding the red flag of burning houses and tires,
lifting your bare fists against armoured cars
you were run over by the wheels of ratels.
How frail is a human body confronted by steel:
yet you walked with a naked face towards machine guns.
For man, destructible as he is, is feared
by contraptions made of steel and blind men.
For there is nothing stronger than this perishable flesh,
when it walks singing towards the weapons of death.
And you walk, you are dead, but you walk:
and your mutilated bodies create terror
among the ruling class.

You spray black paint onto peaceful walls in
                        white suburbia:
RELEASE MANDELA! FREE ALL DETAINEES!
            THE STRUGGLE CONTINUES!
Songs of revolution travel with you into
                        football stadiums.
As you walk through classrooms, students begin
to understand economics and history.
Passing like an ice-cold wind through the boardrooms
the jagged curves of profit tend downwards.
You wait for workers returning late in the evening
to their distant hovels: you talk about courage.

You are the guest of honour in the tin walls
                                    of shanty towns,
they share sparse sugar and tea with you in tents
                                    and cardboard houses.
You who have hanged yourselves in prison cells
council us not to despair but to fight.
You whose brains have been blown out give us advice:
You are hungry, who will give you food?
Don't trust the promises of the rich: they have
                                    betrayed you before.
Nobody will give you food, if your work is not needed
in the current business cycle. Trust only those
who have nothing to give. They will give you food.
Trust only those that have been to jail: they can
                                    set you free.

———

Nostalgia for a Country

Oh, how hard it is
To live this exile
Inside oneself

Oh, how hard it is
To cry for joy
To die freely
In the land of one's Ancestors
Oh heartland
Oh AZANIA
Oh MANDELA

Will you ever know
How many of your children
From the North to the South
From the East to the West
Revere you
And adore you!

Oh, how hard it is
To live this exile
Inside oneself.

(Translated from French by Michael Dewar)

―――

Mandela the African

SURNAME: Soweto – Sharpeville
FIRST NAME: South Africa
MOTHER – FATHER: Azania

I've seen dreams
Broken into pieces
I've seen black flowers
Scythed down in the moonlight

I've seen a mother in tears
A cluster of clouds
Spanning the horrors
I've seen waves of tears
Unfurl onto the continent

I've seen a cow
Devour its offspring one by one
Its milk, a stream
Poured out into faraway seas
Over there in the dawn
Of an illuminated night

I've seen little black angels
Fall like stone
In the streets of Soweto
Of Soweto
Of Soweto
Victims of Apartheid

I've seen wave after wave
Of kamikaze columns
Entire battalions
Their bodies a melée of weapons
Sweeping down upon the white Citadel
Laying siege to the borders of intolerance

I've seen Marx Mandela in all its glory
The new Gospel of Christ
To the body and soul of blacks
Reawakening hope
For the liberation of a martyred people
I've seen MANDELA the crusader
Mandela the courageous
Mandela the incorruptible
Mandela the indomitable
Mandela the Chaka-Zulu
'New look'
Mandela the African
Visiting his troops
To the cheers
And clamour of his people
And the whole world
Was celebrating.

(Translated from French by Michael Dewar)

———

Death by Apathy
Dedicated to Nelson Mandela

Look at the big vulture
Circling above us
There must be something
Rotting around here
It's us my friend
We're dying
Dying of apathy
So don't take your eyes off him
For he's circling too near.

———

Passages: Earth Space

For Nelson Mandela and the Children of Azania

there is no one in the bottom of a champagne bottle
there's no guerrilla waiting with loaded uzi
                    to sail down the san juan river
                            gunning for commandante zero
there's no one to help me free nelson mandela
    or to bring the murderers of victoria mxenge
                to their rightful brutal deaths

the bottom of a champagne bottle is a pitiful
                    American gesture / celebrating dishonestly
        the will to die for freedom
                outside durban or capetown

for south african blacks / champagne is verboten
                (too good for the dirty kaffirs) Azanians

when the ANC marches over botha's
                dried & hate-filled bones / his sinews
        crippled with wickedness / mauled under
        the feet of children whose lives he'd have

wiped out / if it weren't for the mines / diamonds
            & gold / he imagines his skeleton shines
        like gold / his skull on a ray of diamonds /
mind you / he's being crushed as he would
crush angola / as he imagines cabral is silenced /

botha banned
                the marching feet of millions of children
another way to free nelson mandela / to
ban krugerrands as the israelis would obliterate
palestines & mengeles /
                no questions asked / only the skin as evidence
    of heinous crimes or innocence /
    wisdom / there are no freedom fighters armed /
        & ready / chanting

PATRIA O MUERTE

NICARAGUA VENCIA / EL SALVADOR
VENCERA
que viva la liberación de la gente negra
del africa del sur
namibia
angola
grenada
mozambique
quien sabe donde estará / el próximo
territorio libre / no solamente en américa
pero en el mundo /

PATRIA O MUERTE

que viva la liberación mundial
une vie sans oppression
pour toi / para ti / une vie sans
oppression
where the color / the color of our
skin is not evidence of heinous
crimes or innocence.

———

Azania Burns

Mandela, the fire is serious
But not yet hopeless.
You call for assistance
While neighbours bewail,
They have only their tears as water.
Only the fire-starters deign to design
There, behind the water, they cry your name but remark
Mandela, and what if we were to consult Martin Luther King?

(Translated from French by Michael Dewar)

———

Poem to the Southern Wind

And the steps of men keep going
patiently counting the stones of the road
long road on which you
encapsulating the spirit of insurgency
like a light of inspiring brilliance
you rise against the pale destiny
imposed on your mutilated flag

and on days of delayed reason
with them you also
but you always
you only
you friend among men
you MANDELA Nelson
human symbol of permanent voice

your light and your voice
raised up in anticipation of every second
not even the longevity of days
of this seemingly prolonged silence
not even the foolish obsession with your incarceration
can ever destroy
and even less silence

from you the clamour of the southern wind rises
carrying magnanimity to us
the prophecy of certain truth
without time or limit
because your voice is permanent
and is in you my Brother
the sacred body of the gods of our faith.

(Translated from the Portuguese by Richard Bartlett)

Mandela

How does the old man spend his day
In the cage they keep him,
Knowing the wife he left behind,
When bride and bridegroom embraced a flag,
Is no freer beyond the statutory steps
That take her to him, when twice in a year,
They allow her past her garden in Soweto?
Does he, outside the routine drill of the day,
Tell the passing of the day upon
The beat of his slowing heart?
Sitting or asleep on his bed of stone,
What does he see, what does he dream
In the dark of day so slow to break?
Does the old man hear
Above the waves battering Robben Island,
Above the thunder rolling over Drakensberg,
The clamour and clangour of children in revolt,
All ready to die outside their classrooms
Rather than receive the pen
And pit reserved for their parents?
How many times, walking round his cell,
In more than a quarter century of dark,
Has he circled the earth?
And when the concourse of doubt comes crowding him,
As they must during the day,
Crowing to him: 'Can a man lead in solitary?'
'Can he who merges so well with the night of his cell?'
Does the old man then curse his day
He is no dissident,
Incarcerated in another land,
For whom mighty presidents, prime ministers,
Chancellors, primates, editors and dons
Roar forth human rights,
Swear never again to deal with the devil
Until the regime lets his people go?
So many thoughts in a small room!
Before the cameras of the world,
A wall of glass between,

Sit, coupled to telephones, man and woman
Who must not sleep together,
Because of the flag bride and bridegroom embraced
So that they and their children
May look the sun in the face,
Walk erect on earth as given them by God.
Children now are parents since the vow was made.
Oh, cameras in space, hurtling to pierce
Planets in search of light,
In search of life,
Show us the thoughts of an old man kept in a cage
Away from wife,
Away from life!

———

For Mandela

The chokers of "the Resistance" foolishly
watch their hands bleed and swell against the edge
of the struggle, your life, the people
entwined like a three strand rope
tying into a hangman's noose for
the death of apartheid

———

Letter to a Political Prisoner

Behind the fences of barbed wire
Behind iron bars
Locked in your cell
Under the stone walls –
Wherever you are, my friend,
I can see your face.

I send you a towel
Wrapped in olive leaves.
Press it to your eyes
And let the image remain
Embedded forever
In a crucifixion of cloth.

Sometimes, my friend,
When the rain falls in my country
And the upturned faces of my people
Weep towards the sun
I tell them I have seen the sun
In darker places and in catacombs of ice.

I send you my love.
I send you a flag weaved
Without pain or nationality.
I send you my heart
Cradled forever
In a handful of rain.

Sleep well, my friend,
And when they wake you in the morning
Tell them you have slept bone to bone
And mouth to mouth
And stone to stone.
Tell them that you are not alone.

I send you a lamp
I send you my hand raised
Against the bleeding of our kind.
I send you a storm –
Raging forever
Against the iniquities of the blind.

———

Small Passing

*For a woman whose baby died stillborn, and who was told by a man
to stop mourning, "because the trials and horrors suffered daily by
black women in this country are more significant than the loss of one
white child".*

1

In this country you may not
suffer the death of your stillborn,
remember the last push into shadow and silence,
the useless wire and cords on your stomach,
the nurse's face, the walls, the afterbirth in a basin
Do not touch your breasts
still full of purpose.
Do not lie awake at night hearing
the doctor say "It was just as well"
and "You can have another".
In this country you may not
mourn small passings.

See: the newspaper boy in the rain
will sleep tonight in a doorway.
The woman in the busline
may next month be on a train
to a place not her own.
The baby in the backyard now
will be sent to a tired aunt,
grow chubby, then lean,
return a stranger.
Mandela's daughter tried to find her father
through the glass. She thought they'd let her touch him.
And this woman's hands are so heavy when she dusts
the photographs of other children
they fall to the floor and break.
Clumsy woman, she moves so slowly
as if in a funeral rite.

On the pavement the nannies meet.
These are legal gatherings.
They talk about everything, about home,
while the children play among them,
their skins like litmus, their bonnets clean.

2

Small wrists in a grave.
Baby no one carried live
between houses, among trees.
Child shot running,
stones in his pocket,
boy's swollen stomach
full of hungry air.
Girls carrying babies
not much smaller than themselves.
Erosion. Soil washed down to the sea.

3

I think these mothers dream
headstones of the unborn.
Their mourning rises like a wall
no vine will cling to.
They will not tell you your suffering is white.
They will not say it is just as well.
They will not compete for the ashes of infants.
I think they may say to you:
Come with us to the place of the mothers.
We will stroke your flat empty belly,
let you weep with us in the dark,
and arm you with one of our babies
to carry home on your back.

———

from **Elegy For Johnny**

And the voices linked
Ducking and soaring urging him on

Shosholoza Mandela	*Push forward Mandela*
Shay'induku Mfana	*Strike a powerful blow, young man*
Uzokuzwangathi	*You'll be informed by us*
Masekulungile	*When all is well*
Wakal'u – Vervudi	*Verwoerd wept*
Wakal'e – Pitoli	*Wept in Pretoria*
Wathi kuyashisa	*And suffered great hardship*
Ngenxa ka Mandela	*Because of Mandela*

And the door burst open, flinging out fear of the unknown

And the room suddenly shimmered and shone
With the blinding radiance
Of our Prince of Light himself
That rock of intractable courage right there
Before these hunters of freedom
Rolihlahla Nelson Mandela
In full gear holstered for battle
So magnificent
So awesome
So blood-and-body quivering that sight
It is not difficult to understand why
The staunch and faint-hearted alike were to feel
And later say as Mfanafuthi so often repeated
"I almost fainted"
They fainted to wake up new

Alright *Lala S'thandwa*   *Sleep well, Beloved*
Lal'uphumule   *Rest and recover strength*
Yes no more can we hear you
But we shall sing your songs
Must and will sing them madly
through them we touch the soul of diviners
We share the visions of the possessed
For in them live our heroes and heroines
they are inspired and inspire
For to sing them is to be attuned to greatness in tune
We must sing for when we say Rolihlahla
We mean ageless rock
The baobab's petrified centuries of resistance
We mean rock, the moving immovable that moves us
And how and why
Such boulders of righteousness lead and still by example
Direct
Toppling the pillars of the citadel of infamy

(Translation of the isiZulu by Menzi Ndaba)

To Nelson Mandela

(Descending the steps of Humanity. Seeing the dark sea of the errant phenomenon of armed attrition. Feeling with words imprisoned on the lips the perfume of discrimination distributed for a ridiculous price in Durban, Pretoria, Soweto...Seeing in the propagation of sombre signals the design of division and other inspired agonies that keep vigil over us while men step by step ascend the cruel horizon. And so we will rise to the daily tree, daily life, ingredient of our tragedy.)

(Translated from Portuguese by Richard Bartlett)

———

-

There you remain, fettered,
giving us freedom –
your hands wide open.
Today we want you to know
that each feather
on our wings of liberty
bears the imprint of your prison bars;
that we are determined travellers
along the pathways
your capacity inspires;
that from your prison cell
you free and release
those hearts anchored
in indifference,
and with the strength
of your living example
you break the patterns
of agreements,
of resolutions and consensus
that did not respect with integrity
the dignity of each man,
dignity you strive for and proclaim
with your shackles and chains.

*For Nelson Mandela, on
his 70th birthday
(imprisoned for the past
26 years – his only crime:
being born black)*

(Translated from Spanish by Rosemary Wiltshire)

———

To Mandela

In a cell girdled by a sea leaping and crushing
against stone walls:
spraying cold burning water
through the steel bars
where you keep your vigil.

a shower of water and fire
over your head and shoulders,
over your chest, hips and legs:
tall and indestructible
sculptured from the soil of a continent
fired in flames
with spherical clay pots,
arrow tips, and blades;
proofed in furnaces
of the puissant proletariat
and immersed to cool
in rivers and the sea.

Yes, in you
a miraculous mingling
of water and fire.

Your spirit is a seagull soaring
high above the penal island
saturated with the blood of lepers
and the presence
of courageous and enlightened ones.
You comprehend the instincts
of the last surviving seals
mating on the apron of the island,
spilling seed on
the blood-soaked sand.

With a shoal of black and silver fish
you dive to the seabed
where the last faint rays of the sun penetrate
and illuminate the noble face
of Makana who burst into
surf with a plangent cry of freedom
breaking from his lips.

On clear days
the rugged profile of the coast
and distant peaks mark
the vast circumference of a restless hinterland.

You are on the minds of everyone.
In the waves you decipher
the messages
from the struggle you inspired.
At night
stars like distant fires
trace the outlines
and the inner core of your face
defining the distance
between you and universe
in a gesture
pure and irreducible: a clenched fist or a handshake.

Then the water carried you
manacled and guarded
by captors lost in hatred.
In the smoke above the burning peninsula
you see a lifetime: a fleeing moment
persistent and eternal.

Between the harbour and the prison
through the grilled windows
of a truck, a besieged city calling on you
to liberate it.
From your cell the morning star
a pristine eye:
Freedom for all here and now.

———

Xhosa Chief
Nelson Mandela

Then the country was ours...the land, the forests the rivers.

I

The Xhosa Chief says:
here is the boy
of the lambs,
this Transkei boy
who will hold Pretoria captive,
bound only by his daily breath,
waking in the African sun,
lying down in her slip-away arms.
That is how he will win,
this "kaffir,"
this black lion
who loves the veld.

II

What Pretoria must kill
is not simple.
Biko said it was a word:
Amandla!, so they killed Biko.
Children of Soweto said
it was language.
before shooting Soweto boys,
Boer guards ordered:
Raise your fists, shout Amandla!
But only the boys fell.
Now they scrawl *Mandela*
on toilet stalls in Watts,
on prison walls in Manila, Rome, London
where patriots and pimps
mark their claims on destiny's
holding tanks, one
chalked, burned, carved
cry, amidst the foul, raging words.
Mandela is what they scratch.
It is all the pride some have left.

III

At the gate of Lincoln Park Zoo
on Chicago's North side,
gardeners with quilters' eyes
sow patches of purple astor –aster–
twirls of marigold,
a circle of white geraniums
hover like moths, above
the mossy lawn. Trim.
Inside, in a new steel cage,
a languid lion places one
great paw after another,
silent, indifferent, as if
walking were a royal gesture.
He's dangerous, the white boys say.
The black girls rode two buses
from the South Side where
rivers of broken glass
run chippy over tin cans,
under abandoned cars,
glitter beneath a white neon moon.
Call that bad boy Mandela,
say the girls, he like a caged king, too.

IV

In 1964 Mandela spoke:
"It is an ideal for which
I am prepared to die."
As if the message were delayed,
the young ask: What did he say, Mamma?
Say that, Mandela, even in chains?
In the West, where faith is not easy,
the prophecy repeats over and over,
this Transkei boy
they could not kill him.

_____

Ah! Rolihlahla!!

Fellow Africans, we are not by this Song starting a war cry.
But we felt you had to hear a thing or two about this son of the
House of Ngubengcuka.

A man, they say, usually lives up to his name,
And this is only too true when such is of royal birth.

Though you were of a minor house, the iXhiba
Jongintaba picked you

Brought you to the Royal Home
To the house of No-Inglani, his wife
The woman with the long breast, daughter of Krune,
To the Royal Home, fount of the culture
And custom of a people
The Royal Home where the art of service
To the nations is learnt.
And when he initiated you into manhood
He saluted you with the name "Rolihlahla"
Full knowing that such a bough sometimes
Bristles with thorns
Even those of the thistle and the thornbush.

A mere youth, you left home for eGoli
eGoli where man has no worth
eGoli where he who prided himself
On his humanhood now becomes just a Kaffir
eGoli where the sjambok of the white man
Lashes indiscriminately the commoner
And him of royal birth.
Amazed, shocked, you protested
Young calf of the royal herd
For such you had never known before
You were nurtured and taught
That Man was a noble being
Full of dignity, humanity and grace
And as such worthy of respect.

Soon your voice was heard among the youth
Condemning and protesting such treatment
At first, we were not impressed
Dismissing it as the gallantry of an angry young man
His blood hot with the fervour of youth,
A baby teething, blowing to cool his gums
"He is of the House of Hala," we said
"The Hala, cowards among the nations
Where then would he get such courage?"
We were missing the truth, however,
That a man will follow his father's cattle
Take something from his mother's people;
For, is he not the son of Nosekeni of the ama-Mpemvu
The ama-Mpemvu, Masters of Ceremony
In the courtyards of the House of Phalo?

It was at eGoli, you met the woman
Of the ama-Qwathi, daughter of Mase
You were both young; you a youthful dandy.
She groomed and molded you;
Nurtured and cultivated you
As a mother her child;
She inspired and encouraged you,
So, today you are expert in the White Man's law
And in the affairs of the nation, among the best.
And when her task was done
She turned you over to the nation, saying:
"There he is, my people. He is yours!
You called him 'Rolihlahla'
I will remain behind in the house
Rearing for you his offspring
Thembilile, Makgatho and Makaziwe."
How then, can the nation not give thanks
To you daughter of the ama-Qwathi?

So saying she entrusted you to the Mpondo woman
Nomzamo, the high-spirited, unbridled
bold daughter of the House of Ngutyana
Who, on arrival said: "Fear not Madiba;
I am here already;
I'll pull out of your feet even the hardest of thorns.
Treading in your footsteps
I'll be your eyes, your ears, your defender;
Pull along this bough, son of the House of Hala
Even though bristling with thorns, bring it along
Your people are as a lamb caught in the thistle bush
They cannot breathe;
They know not where to turn.
When they try to move, it is: 'Go back! Go Back!'
When they try to settle down, it is: 'Not here!
Not here!! Not here!!!'"

Then it was you threw yourself
Into the struggle
The struggle for the liberation of your people.
Soon your presence was noted;
From all sides, young men and women
Sang: "Slink in the shadows, Mandela
Hitting hard with your stick."
Said this to one who wielded that stick well
In the plains of Qweqwe and Mqhekezweni
To an adept at surprising and challenging
The youth of Qunu and Qokolweni.
"Slink in the shadows, Mandela,
Hit hard with your stick.
You will hear from us when we are ready."

You wielded that stick well, son of Henry
On that day in the law court;
Brought out all the facts, for all to see.
Everything was clear, as clear as day.
Even the blind could see, and the deaf hear.
This was the day the regime was accusing
You of high treason.
Madiba, you spoke without fear or favour
"I have heard the wailing of my people,
My people groaning under the yoke of oppression,
A people chewing the bread of despair,
And drinking the waters of damnation.
My people whose cry is not heeded
By the government under which we serve.

"That cry tore the very guts of my being.
I remembered that our forefathers
Died, fighting to save this land;
It was taken from them through guile
And at the barrel of the gun;
Even, when they laid down their arms
It was not to accept defeat,
But to recoup after a battle lost
With the knowledge that through war
And blood, it would be regained
by us, the future generation.
So it was, I said to my comrades
A change of course, my countrymen
The time has come to regain our land
We, and we alone can do it
I swear by the House of Hala
No bull has ever been driven
Out of its own cattle-fold
Your Worship, if this truth be treason.
So be it. I am prepared to die."

Awu: What a day noble sons
And daughters of Afrika!!
The day when this boy Henry spoke.
Spoke, and our hair stood on end!!
The boy grew, grew in stature
Before our very eyes!
He stood tall; towered over all those Giants of Law
In that courtroom
And these words: "Your worship, if this truth be
treason
So be it. I am prepared to die."
Struck home in the minds of those with a conscience
And the pure of heart.

He damned and confounded his accusers.
The regime was at a loss;
They did not know what to do.
At first, they considered sentencing him to death;
Pondered and retreated,
Remembering that the truth does not die
With the one who spoke it.
The truth cannot be hanged.
And his final words in that law court
Had filled the four corners of the world.
Then, they sentenced him to life in prison
Hoping thereby to bury him alive
Forgetting that the truth defies even the grave.

Your words in that law court that day
Remained forever in the minds of your people
Today they are repeated by children of yesterday;
Children who never saw or knew you,
But know of you as one of the heroes
In the struggle for freedom.
People, today, throughout the world are clamouring
"Release Mandela and all those others
You've confined on Robben Island".
Even these valleys are calling: "Release Mandela"
The very mountains echo it: "Release Mandela"
It is ceaseless clamour
That has puzzled the regime to no end.

"Let him renounce violence
We will release him," said the wily jackal
"The ball is in your court," was your reply.
"For it is you who holds the keys to open
These doors."
Renounce violence?
How can I when my people
Are still bound hand and foot,
Their voices hoarse with crying
With no one heeding that cry?
What man has ever sold his birthright
For a mess of pottage?
How can my people begin to talk with you
When they are held in bondage?
Open the doors so that we, too, may come in,
Where, we, too, will formulate the laws
To govern our land...
Give our best for the good of our land
Just as our forefathers were wont to do.

Madiba, your people out here have had enough!
They seem to want to say: "Give the word, Madiba
Make the call! Only those who dare ever win
Death is harsh; death is cruel.
No doubts still linger; all fear is gone
We are waiting on you to give the word.
Move stealthily, Mandela; slink in the shadows
Hitting hard with your stick
Hear us now; we are ready
To take on the enemy!"

Don't leave Xhamele behind, the light-skinned
Son of Sisulu;
It is he who will command the flank
On the day of battle.
He is Qwathi, the Qwathi who bear
No wound on the backs of their heads.
Bring along that Zizi of the house of Jama
Govan Mbeki of Mpukane is his name
He will be the long staff with which
We test the waters of the deep pools
On the day we cross over.
It is he also who will teach and guide us
In the ways of governing and living
In the new land,
The land of freedom, equality and humanity.

The son of Mhlaba and the son of Mlangeni
Will be your defending stick
With which you ward off the enemy.
With the son of Motsoaledi as your long stick
You will feel out and draw the enemy;
For close combat, pull out your short stick
The son of Kathrada.
Come to us surrounded by those hundreds,
Of our people they've confined on that Island
It is by their company, we will recognise you
When, united, we come out to meet
And welcome you
All coming to tell our oppressors
"We are of the kraal manure;
We are of this soil,
This is our LAND!
OPEN THE DOOR!!"

(Translated from Xhosa)

———

Ode to My Father

Tata

I can imagine

> what you would be
> if I was not
> what you would say
> if I kept quiet

I can imagine

where you would go
> if I remained
> where you would end
> if I started

I can imagine

> what you would admire
> if I was disgusted
> what you would love
> if I only hated

I can imagine

> when you would die
> if I lived
> when you would cry
> if I laughed

I can imagine

> what you would enjoy
> if I felt depressed
> what you would do
> if I did not

———

The Ballad of Robben Island Gaol

"Being free is something only a man knows: only the man who
behaves inside a dungeon as if he already were free"
                                                    Miguel Hernández

The little birds put to sleep the dreams of Mandela
who had forgotten the taste of saltpetre
the freshness of the sky, the splendours of the desert.
A giant shadow took over the mountains,
The sober land of the Transkei
And let out the violent howl of a carrion beast.
Since then an immemorial prisoner
sings to the ochres of the island
from his cell…
In a burning summer
his hands found relief in the oasis
his beloved would bring him.
They had enclosed him so much
that he could not hear the wind on the reefs,
nor the murmuring breath of the grasses,
nor could he see the sun,
nor the ring of the moon shining on high.
They kept him in solitary confinement
and they did the unspeakable to cut out his tongue,
to tie his feet and hands
even bound his heart.
Mandela, next to the songs of waves and birds,
opened furrows in the earth
and irrigated them with the water of his mouth.
Without leaving his cell,
he sees everything, he touches everything,
he turns everything into an arrow against the red-hot steel
of his bitter gaolers.
From a little-known corner
he continues to throw out his flower of love of country
through the meadows of Namibia,
over the coasts of Cape Town,
over the bloodied asphalt of Johannesburg,
among the bodies of the Angolan bond-rebels,

over Guinea and the Congo,
over Nubia and Carthage,
over the archipelagos of the Indian Ocean
and the immense waters of the Nile
Mandela flew over his cell
to sing this ballad
of Robben Island Gaol

(Translated from Spanish by Jean Andrews)

Can I Get a Witness Here

How shall I tell them at home
That I met you at Grenoble
Beneath the slopes of the snow-capped Alps
Father Nelson Mandela

How can I make anyone believe
That the streets were full of you
In Grenoble outside the gates of Pollsmoor Prison
Father Nelson Mandela

Who can help tell everyone how your face
Loomed large in a city older than your country
Dressed warmly in a polo-neck jersey
Father Nelson Mandela

You stood far from the Koeberg nuclear station
Yet so very near the French nuclear power monster
Enclosed within the majestic towering Alps
Father Nelson Mandela

Up there on the slopes on the Alps
A thousand feet up the tumbling green slopes
I stood looking at the city below
Pondering the meaning of a place
Unwashed for centuries
A Roman abode in times past
At peace with itself
No fusses of centenary celebrations
Whose yield demeans the human heart
With such guilt as Operation Hunger
Amidst the glitter of gold and diamonds
I was standing where I could pluck off clouds
The air was a fresh green smell
Clean
Neat
Pure
All around there was the cherry-tree in bloom
With lily-white flowers
All around there was the apple-tree in bloom
With dazzling pink flowers
All around there was a mass of pine-trees
Stubbornly green all seasons
As defiant as the massive rocks
And the high peaks of the Alps
Wearing white caps all seasons
And then all at once I felt a moving spirit
My heart's pounding beat
In unison with the enthralling sights about me
The ring of rugged timeless mountains
The rolling green sides of these high sentinels
And oh! I saw the serene face of
Father Nelson Mandela
As if indifferent to the words scrolled
Over and below his sublime face
In a bleeding red colour
                    LIBEREL MANDELA
I asked
As if in between the tears and supplication
of a mother

Why Lord
Why are the screams of men across the whole face of the earth
Unheard
Unheeded
Unmoving
Are you one or several

———

Your Logic Frightens Me, Mandela

Your logic frightens me, Mandela
Your logic frightens me. Those years
Of dreams, of time accelerated in
Visionary hopes, of savouring the task anew,
The call, the tempo primed
To burst in supernovae round a 'brave new world'!
Then stillness. Silence. The world closes round
Your sole reality; the rest is … dreams?

Your logic frightens me.
How coldly you disdain legerdemains!
'Open Sesame' and – two decades' rust on hinges
Peels at the touch of a conjurer's wand?
White magic, ivory-topped black magic wand,
One moment wand, one moment riot club
Electric cattle prod and whip or sjambok
Tearing flesh and spilling blood and brain?

This bag of tricks, whose silk streamers
Turn knotted cords to crush dark temples?
A rabbit punch sneaked beneath the rabbit?
Doves metamorphosed in milk-white talons?
Not for you the olive branch that sprouts
Gun muzzles, barbed-wire garlands, tangled thorns
To wreathe the brows of black, unwilling Christs.

Your patience grows inhuman, Mandela.
Do you grow food? Do you make friends
Of mice and lizards? Measure the growth of grass
For time's unhurried pace?
Are you now the crossword puzzle expert?

Chess? Ah, no! Subversion lurks among
Chess pieces. Structured clash of black and white,
Equal ranged and paced? An equal board? No!
Not on Robben Island. Checkers? Bad to worse.
That game has no respect for class or king-serf
Ordered universe. So, Scrabble?

Monopoly? Now, that …! You know
The game's modalities, so do they.
Come collection time, the cards read 'Whites Only'
In the Community Chest. Like a gambler's coin
Both sides heads or tails, the 'Chance' cards read:
Go to jail. Go straight to jail. Do not pass 'GO'.
Do not collect a hundredth rand. Fishes feast,
I think, on those who sought to by-pass 'GO'
On Robben Island.

Your logic frightens me, Mandela, your logic
Humbles me. Do you tame geckos?
Do grasshoppers break your silences?
Bats' radar pips pinpoint your statuesque
Gaze transcending distances at will?
Do moths break wing
Against a light bulb's fitful glow
That brings no searing illumination?
Your sight shifts from moth to bulb,
Rests on its pulse-glow fluctuation –
Are kin feelings roused by a broken arc
Of tungsten trapped in vacuum?

Your pulse, I know, has slowed with earth's
Phlegmatic turns. I know your blood
Sagely warms and cools with seasons,
Responds to the lightest breeze
Yet scorns to race with winds (or hurricanes)
That threaten change on tortoise pads.

Is our world light-years away, Mandela?
Lost in visions of that dare supreme
Against a dire supremacy of race,
What brings you back to earth? The night guard's
Inhuman tramp? A sodden eye transgressing through
The Judas hole? Tell me Mandela,
That guard, is he your prisoner?

Your bounty threatens me, Mandela, that taut
Drumskin of your heart on which our millions
Dance. I fear we latch, fat leeches
On your veins. Our daily imprecisions
Dull keen edges of your will.
Compromises deplete your act's repletion –
Feeding will-voided stomachs of a continent,
What will be left of you, Mandela?

———

Like Rudolf Hess, The Man Said!

'We keep him (Mandela) for the same reason the Allied Powers
are holding Rudolf Hess.'
— Pik Botha, South African Foreign Minister

Got you! Trust the Israelis.
I bet they flushed him out, raced him down
From Auschwitz to Durban, and Robben Island.
Mandela? Mandel ...Mendel ...Mengel ...Mengele!
It's he! Nazi superman in sneaky blackface!

A brilliant touch – let's give the devil his due.
Who would seek the Priest of Vivisections
Masquerading as a Black-and-Proud?
No living heart in mouth, one step ahead
Those Jew-vengeance squads.
Safe on Robben Island, paratroops of Zion
Bounty hunters, frogmen, crack Z squads,
Wiesenthal fanatics – here you'll find
Robben Island is no Entebbe. This pogrom maestro
Has his act together – he'll serve time
To spit on borrowed time!

A cunning touch, those modest body counts
In Sharpeville, Soweto. In your heydays,
The crop was tens of thousands. Now who would once
Surmise the mastermind directing death
In tens? Or twenties? Even hundreds!

In your luxurious island home, outfitted
State-of-the-art laboratory, ideas
Flow out to pay the state in kind – protection
For caste research, food for thought.
the ninety-day detention law – your idea?
A ninety-day laboratory per man.
blackened cells – not padded, no –
You diagnosed inferior minds, not madness. Cells
So lightproof, even the stereotypic eyes
Shed their white pretence – Black is Beautiful?
You made them taste sublimity in Blacked-Out
Solitary.

You listened to their minds go loudly awry.
Mere operational change, from flaying live;
'Improving' on those naïve tries of nature.
Do you feel nostalgia for the past?
Stripping the 'circumcised dogs' to buff and
Searching secret parts for jewellery? And your love
For gold teeth – ah yes, gold!
Gassed them cold and questioned their anatomy.
Too bad some woke midsurgery,
But you swung the pendulum the other way
And thousands died from greedy inhalation –
They loved the stuff, they died laughing, no?

Gold! They wore their ransom in their teeth
Their dowry, tithes, death duties. But –
No need here for that painful dentistry,
Assaying the yellow fire even before
The body is cold. Our Broederland
Flaunts the gold standard of the world.
Black muscles work it – quickly you adjusted –
None but racial slanderers now predict
A genocide. Modestly you shun the Final Solution –
Who slays the goose that lays such golden eggs?

The gold exposed you. Bloodhound Jews
Whose mouth you quarried for your pay –
Your passion tasting still of blood –
Set their burgled gums to track you down
To the golden tip of the black continent.

Cute Mandgela, sought everywhere,
Cooly ensconced on Robben Island.
I saw your hand in Biko's death, that perfect
Medical scenario, tailormade for you.
And hundreds more of young Icarus syndrome –
Flying suspects, self-propelled
From fifty-storey floors
To land on pavements labelled – WHITES ONLY!
You question them only in white preserves –
How would a high-rise building fit in shantytown?

So desperate for acceptance, exhibitionist,
Made omelette of their brains for white
Rights of passage. Sheer sophistry! Skin
Is deep enough. Your lancet Mandgele, was genius,
Creator hand so deft, made anaesthetic
Optional – blue cornea graft, heart-liver swap,
Organic variants – eye in earholes, leg to armpit,
Brain transfer – all child's play to you, but –
Not even you could work a whole-skin graft.
A thousand dead in the attempt
Makes proof enough – wouldn't you say?

Mendgela's in town – the word is passed.
Keep park benches sanitised. White is white
(Though sometimes Jew but – times do change.) –
Black is red is commie menace
Red is what we see when Icarus leaps
A red-forked lightning from cloud-hugging floors,
Tight-lipped, fork-tongued, terror mentors,
Beclouding issues clearly black and white.

And the racial traitors – white Ruth First,
Opens a letter in Harare – *Boom!* – Alibied,
You smile on Robben. Too bad, re coloured Brutus,
Mister *Boots, Knuckles and Bones*. Too athletic?
Caught a bullet but it missed the vital organs
Trying to beat us to the Olympic laurels.
Hassling, hounding Bundbroederland from sports
Our lifeblood, proof of stock and breeding –
Cowards! Like their new uneasy allies –
Those back-stabbing, 'trading partners' –
Scared of competition? Of open contest? Right!
We have the carats; keep your plated medals!

Gold! Ah yes, Mandela-Hess,
You got us in this mess. The Allied Powers
Rightly hold you pacing wall to wall,
Treading out your grand designs
In commie jackboots. Mandela-Mengele,
You are ours! We'll keep you close.
Your *Doppelgänger* haunts us to the vaults.
Yes, 'thars gold in them thar mountains' – would *you*
Let Mandela loose?

———

To Nelson Mandela

Forgive me for succumbing
To a most
Counter-revolutionary of ills:
The cult of personality!
I am a simple man
Of flesh and dreams
Hardened by dashed hopes
And sore bones
The callouses of our shared home

(The Pollsmoor land that unravels
From Limpopo to Cape Point
Day after day after day
My windows open, yours shut)
Don't blame me for succumbing
when another simple man,
African, father, poet like myself
Comes strolling from a cesspool
With an unbowed head
Roaring like a lion
With a smile as gentle as the dawn

Forgive me for succumbing to this most
counter-revolutionary of ills.

———

Birth Day Party
(for Nelson Mandela)

No cake
No new wish
            Years of blowing out candle fires of hate
No tightness in your belly from overeating delectables now chest now
Trunk filled w/tuberculosis
Yet, on this 70th year
            the corners of your soul turn upward in a knowing smile
Knowing the pulse of the world drums a prelude to a real celebration,
            the Birth Day of freedom in South Africa

Freedom band playin' for the party
            Price is high but they jam non-stop
Syncopated riffs of sighing
            soaring past high notes of suffering
Shake shake
            rattling of rock throwing warriors' dry bones
            rising to clothe themselves in freedom dust

Shrivelled, humpbacked grieving Earth Mamas/Widows
            put on their last pat of powder, oils, chalk, dyes or red mud
            They swing out of their mourning clothes to Dawn
                Dawning multicoloured beaded jewellery and
                                            tattered yellowed
                handmade lace of pride
            Come dance, Mamas, dance
                Dance on the moist fertile grounds of
                                            self-determination
                It's party time!

Folks be comin' from all over
Your silky brown skinned queen, Warrior Winnie
            stands firm at your door
            waiting for part of her soul to return

Caribbean aunties, African uncles,
South American cousins
and North American brothers and sisters

They be flyin', walkin', runnin', swimmin' and show-boatin'
        to the center of themselves
                to be seen at this Birth Day party

You feast on your favourite prison food
                Fried hopes dipped in corn-a-plenty batter
                Stewed dreams seasoned
                        w/freshly ground Black pepper wake-up nuts
Pit bar-b-que Botha-apartheid burning: and a full tomorrow
                cooked slow and easy on scorching coals of enlightenment
                        havin' been basted w/the drippings of human suffering
                                and rotated on a sure nuff dignified history stick

Folks be guzzlin' grapes of wrath wine
Sippin' from the fountain of
                "LOVE YOUR CHILDREN BETTER THAN YOURSELF"
                home brew
And savourin' Black lightnin'
                100 proof positive of a prosperous future

Folks be just a sweatin'
                been a labourin' a lifetime side by side
                        trying to plant crops in bad soil
Sweat drippin' folks
                banned to a party in an imperfect world
Sweat drippin' but
                determined to perfume each other
                        w/the alluring sweetness of human kindness
                                while they slow dance to a new tune

The Birth Day gift?
                The world's heart, Nelson
                wrapped w/Black, brown, yellow, white and red people
                tied w/a ribbon of melted South African gold and diamonds
An ornate package of squirming humanity on best behaviour
                Careful not to step on anyone's toes

                        ——

A Poem for Nelson Mandela

Here where I live it is Sunday.
From my room I hear black
children playing between houses
and the El at a Sabbath rattle.
I smell barbecue from every direction
and hear black hands tolling church bells,
hear wind hissing through elm trees
through dry grasses

        On a rooftop of a prison
in South Africa Nelson Mandela
tends garden and has a birthday,
as my Jamaican grandfather in Harlem, New York
raises tomatoes and turns ninety-one.
I have taken touch for granted: my grandfather's hands,
his shoulders, his pyjamas which smell of vitamin pills.
I have taken a lover's touch for granted,
recall my lover's touch from this morning
as Mandela's wife pulls memories through years
and years

        My life is black and filled with fortune.
Nelson Mandela is with me because I believe
in symbols; symbols bear power; symbols demand
power; and that is how a nation
follows a man who leads from prison
and cannot speak to them. Nelson Mandela
is with me because I am a black girl
who honors her elders, who loves
her grandfather, who is a black daughter
as Mandela's daughters are black
daughters. This is Philadelphia
and I see this Sunday clean.

———

Testament For The First Accused:
Nelson Mandela For The Twenty-Seven Years

I know Patrice Lumumba had been sometime dead,
and Sylvanus Olympio only just,
though I'm not sure why,
As I try to re-connect myself with my child's mind,
and the memories of events that jumble there –
A knowledge of our distant world, pieced together,
through overheard conversations
and voices on the radio.

In 1962 the world was a very different place:

I didn't know where Montgomery was,
but I'd learnt the meaning of boycott.
Didn't understand Mau Mau,
except it taught the impact of lies,
and what all freedoms cost.
I remember your name, and vague talk of a trial,
and treason being a serious thing;
Sisulu and Mbeki, Goldberg and Mhlaba,
Kathrada, Motsoaledi and Mlangeni, at Rivonia.
These names I have learnt through the years,
but at the time, what I recall for sure,
Is Abebe Bikila's second Olympic Gold,
And Cassius Clay proving he was the greatest,
By the time you made your statement,
And disappeared.

We have not seen you since.

I didn't mark your fiftieth birthday,
but in Ghana J.B. Danquah was already dead,
and we had lived through coups
and countercoups already,
at the start of a second republic.
While Baldwin warned of *The Fire Next Time*,
the White Rhodesians declared UDI,
and the Zimbabweans braced for war.
But we were killing our brothers already in Biafra,
while the whole world watched,
and a young Christopher Okigbo reminded us
that even the poets were dying.
And you were still alive,
And you were still not free.

Though James Brown danced us off the streets,
And "Soul came to Soul" in Ghana,
No one remembered Paul Robeson, and
Mahalia Jackson sung her last.
Singing "We Shall Overcome",
Through frustrated Freedom summers we left
Mississippi, Watts, and Newark burning –
And Medgar, Malcolm and Martin dead. All dead.
And you were still alive,
And you were still not free.

In an angry and lonely world,
we marked the passage of your tenth year
reading *Letters to Martha*, and *Soledad Brother*.
All "Souls were on Ice"
As Arthur Nortje killed himself in an Oxford room,
and an exiled Kabaka died.
We freed Angela Davis, but, on your desolate island,
You were still alive,
And you were still not free.

Your sixtieth birthday reminded us
"This struggle was your life".
But by then, your life had become our struggle
as we buried Hector Petersen,
and a hundred slaughtered children
on the scorched streets of Soweto.
With a jailed Thandi Modisi
We "Cried Freedom" for a murdered Steven Biko,
People young enough to be your children,
And children younger than your children, dead,
So many of them dead.
Yet you at least were still alive,
But you were still not free.

We shouted Frelimo and another empire fell,
Antonio Jacinto "*Survived Tarrafal*",
But Agostinho Neto was dead.
Eduardo Mondlane had been many years murdered,
And we have since mourned the wreckage
of Samora Machel
On the South African side of Mozambique's mountains,
And you were still alive,
And you were still not free.

By your twentieth year,
Anwar Sadat had sued for peace in the Knesset,
And had been later killed for his pains.
And Haile Sellassie the Lion of Judah, had disappeared
Leaving no memorial, except a three thousand year
Imperial kingdom, now decades at war.
And in Eritrea, Tigre, the Sudan, the Spanish Sahara,
The "Harvest of our Dreams" "Reaped a Whirlwind"
of nightmares
And we searched for Janani Luwum
amongst Kampala's martyred.
Marley, who sang for Manley and Mugabe,
was so young dead
But you were still alive,
And you were still not free.

The decades bring the deaths of leaders,
the power and the myth that was Nkrumah
lie broken, like his shattered statue
On the Accra streets.
And in the same week that Jomo Kenyatta
"Faced his sacred Mount Kenya" for the final time,
Kofi Busia's *Challenge to Africa*
in Search of Democracy
Ended. All your peers dead.
But you were still alive,
And you were still not free.

Yet, on a continent being "liberated" "redeemed",
"revolutionised",
Proclaiming "Uhuru", the people were marching.
Twenty-five years after Sharpeville, we march –
Ten years after Soweto, we march.
And when they killed mothers and babies
On their march through Mamelodi,
Still, with them, we march,
For you were still alive,
And you were still not free.

By the time we reached your seventieth birthday,
Another generation of children
Had learned to call your name.
We carry old images of your face, in our hearts,
And on the T-shirts on our backs,
As an icon of a new morning.
The Tembu warrior prince, the lawyer-activist,
The prisoner.
Around the world we marched in our millions,
Demanding your return into this troubled world,
So sadly bereft of heroes,
For you were still alive,
And you were still not free.

You disappeared from our view,
in a world which had taken no small step on the moon
for man;
no Apollos, no Challengers, no Salyuts.
No photographs of the furthest planets,
no walks in space.
The small steps taken on earth for mankind
had included
No Flower Power Love concerts in Woodstock,
No One Love Peace concerts in Kingston, Jamaica
No Art Against Apartheid freedom concerts in Sun City,
No Bands in Aid proclaiming "We are the World".
That world had known no "Cultural Revolution" in China,
No drafted U.S. troops in Vietnam,
No "Killing Fields" in Cambodia.
No vanished *Prisoner Without a Name*
in a *Cell Without a Number*, mourned by the
Mothers of the Plaza de Mayo – And through this all
You were still alive,
And you were still not free.

And now it is the Lord's Day,
the eleventh of February 1990,
And it is five a.m. in Los Angeles, California,
It is eight a.m. in New York and Kingston, Jamaica,
It is one p.m. in Stockholm, London, and Accra, Ghana,
And half the marching world has paused –
To keep vigil,
For it is three p.m. in Cape Town, South Africa,
And we wait to see your face.
After twenty-seven years of fighting, marching
and singing
We keep a ninety-minute watch;
To see you take these next few steps
On this, your *No Easy Walk*
To our uncertain *Freedom*;
To witness your release into this changing world,
Unceasingly, the same.
For you are still alive,
But we are still not free.
Amandla Mandela,
A Luta Continua.

———

Release, February 1990

He emerged, walked free
looking like an ordinary, sweet grandfather
from the Eastern Cape:
those lovely old men we children knew
were wise and saintly,
walking down the streets
in ancient suits, greatcoats
from the First World War. We always greeted,
an exchange both courteous and right.

Grown older, we salute Mandela.
Not the bogeyman, whose face
was a forbidden sight (abroad,
we looked in libraries); nor charismatic
warrior, giving tongue in blood and flame.

The heavens did not fall.
But then, for days before, the mountain
(struck by lightning) burned,
the dark alive with crimson snakes
writhing on air, black elevation of the night.

Confirmation came
less from our eyes, watching the images that flew
about the world, than from the way we felt:
elated, cool, not doubting this was true,
the destined time and place.

This is the way messiahs come –
when time can stand no more delay,
and people throng the streets, mill in the square,
climb trees to see.
                         Even the soldiers
nervous in the mob (since they alone are armed,
and so not free) are part of the convergence,
the dislocated, sudden calm of knowing:
This was the way it had to be.

———

Praise Poems of the
African National Congress

*"They have been through fire and steel, they have
conversed with stones"*

— Yannis Ritsos: *Romiosyne*

I.

Our shouts are peaks in a range of voices;
Our hands shape power in streets of strength;
Our comrades are a million men and women.

For twenty-six years they lived
entombed alive.
They conversed with stones
and the chains that shackled them
shackled thirty million of us.
They walked through the furnace,
they measured distance by roadblock,
and time by section twenty-nine.

their names:	comrade organiser
	comrade delegate
	comrade rank and file.
their address:	here. somewhere.
	Pollsmoor. Victor Verster.
their meals:	tension & cigarettes
their personal lives:	minutes between committees & agenda
their love-making:	under matters arising
their destiny:	death
	– and our liberation.

II.

the new tsars ride by helicopter
the arrogant arm points:
"Kruispad; Khayalitsha –
van daar tot daar…"   *from there to there*

& it is done.

this epoch's cossacks
ride hippos, buffels,
use guns not swords
gas not knouts;
the whips remain whips.
& in Langa, KwaThema, Mamelodi
upon the dust of our roads
red blotches became our shrouds.

Our ghettos are loaded onto lorries:
beds, pots, corrugated iron;
exiled by warlords,
banished to Babylon.
For the hands that shape metal,
steer machines,
for daily commuters of the abyss
who hew gold four kilometres down
suffocating in the inferno;
for our workers:
– the compound
– the firings
– the "disappearance".

Our comrades travel door upon door,
defying fear and fatigue:

strengthening people,
building organisation:
                    – COSAW
                    – COSATU
                    – ANC

& when they are seized
by the Civil Cooperation Bureau
– Siphiwo Mtimkulu, Mathew Goniwe,
Griffiths & Victoria Mxenge –
their bodies lie "cooperated"
through the streets of our land.

III.
Ah! Madiba!

Izwi labantu!	voice of the people
Ikhakha lenkhululeko!	shield of freedom
Umkhonto weSizwe!	spear of the nation

Wazalwa uyinkosana, wena wajika wangabantu:
Born Prince, you became the people
Mfundi, ungumfundisi wetitshala zakho;
Student, you taught your teachers;
Lutsha, ungumququzeleli weenkonde;
Youth Wing, you organised the Elders;
Mphati, wamatshantliziyo awuluthobelanga ucalu-calulo;
Volunteer-in-Chief, you defied apartheid;
Mlandeli wecharter, wazibhengeza ezi nkululeko;
Charterist, you proclaim these Freedoms;
Mmangalelwa, utyholwa ngokungcatsha isizwe osithandayo;
Trialist, they call your patriotism treason;
Mguquli wamajele, wakway amazambane;
Prison reformer, you boycotted potatoes;
Mhambi, uyityhutyhil' iAfrica;
Envoy, you traveled through Africa;
Msebenzi mgodini, urhubuluze phantsi komhlaba;
Gold miner, you work underground;
Gqwetha, usilwele isizwe;
Lawyer, you defend the nation;
Mmangalelwa, uwuphakamisile umthetho;
Accused, you indict the law;
Banjwa, umbambile urhulumente.
Captive, you held a government captive!

mayibuye!   audience: iAfrika!   let it return
masibuye!   let us return
makabuye: let him return
Nelson Rolihlahla ManDEEEEEEEla!
Rolihlahla amaaaaaaaaaaaaaaaaaaaDEla!
AMAAAAAAAAAAAAAAAAADELA!
ncincilili.

(Translation of Xhosa by Sandile Dikeni)

———

from **The Cure at Troy**

"...in February 1990, while I was buried in the depths of Widener
Library in Harvard, hurrying to get a passable version of the play
[The Cure at Troy] into shape for the summer, Nelson Mandela
walked out of the depths of his long imprisonment and into his des-
tiny as leader and reconciler, an intervention by somebody out of the
ordinary, a miraculum that would issue in an administration. The
marooned man, the betrayed one, without the aid of divine fiat, but
with a trust that we share a common human sympathy and dignity,
went on to win the city.

"So in these extraordinary circumstances, I did something pre-
sumptuous: I wrote an extra set of lines for the Chorus. I was able to
invest these lines with a high and hopeful note because they are not,
after all, spoken by me but by the Chorus as representative of all our
hope; and moreover ... there were good reasons why at that moment I
could allow the caution of the first person singular "I" to be sub-
sumed in the surge of conviction coursing first person plural of the
Chorus and the whole world."

Extract from Seamus Heaney's graduation address to Rhodes University,
Grahamstown, South Africa, 2002.

CHORUS:
Human beings suffer
They torture one another
They get hurt and get hard.
No poem or play or song
Can fully right a wrong
Inflicted and endured.

The innocent in gaols
Beat on their bars together.
A hunger-striker's father
Stands in the graveyard dumb.
The police widow in veils
Faints at the funeral home.

History says, *Don't hope*
On this side of the grave.
But then, once in a lifetime
The longed-for tidal wave
Of justice can rise up,
And hope and history rhyme.

So hope for a great sea-change
On the far side of revenge.
Believe that a further shore
Is reachable from here.
Believe in miracles
And cures and healing wells.

Call miracle self-healing:
The utter, self-revealing
Double-take of feeling.
If there's fire on the mountain
Or lightning and storm
And a god speaks from the sky

That means someone is hearing
The outcry and the birth-cry
Of new life at its term.

———

Mandela's Freedom

Mandela wanted freedom
Whites wanted to kill him
Mandela wanted Africa to rule,
The whites wouldn't keep their cool.
He went to jail 27 years whole
Now the whites of Africa woe & wail.

———

from **Rap 25** in **Horns for Hondo**

i feel the cold of a fridge
stone-treading this long bridge
trying to close this gap
that grows to a wider gape
a wound in the heart of a nation
refusing to bow to medication
from man to man an angry wave
blowing man to an early grave
man wields the hammer of security
to stamp & seal his inhumanity
declaring war against time's turning tide
to stay on the profit ride
i'm run down to the verge of calamity
chasing the shadow of amity
o death come topple my plight
visit me like a dream in the night
& i would never wake
if only to ease my ache
turn me into a bed for dew & frost
if only to make man defrost
to come rolling down at last
to relegate tyranny to the past
behold from the skies power comes like rain
to nourish seeds of pain
stretched out runs the fire
dressed in a wire
to stop maputo
coming to soweto
bloodhounds on the tracks of frelimo
tear it to fatten renamo
this is a mongrel state
of uncertain fate
it's a disease for sure
to which we've found a cure
as we trudge forward
against the coward
from the shores of mau mau
to the bushes of frelimo

suckled on the breast of nujoma
graduates of the school of mandela
from the muddy pound
to the bloody rand
aligned devils cower
as we march to power

———

haiku 112 (for Mandela)

emerging from jail
their dragon/our butterfly
his smile is so huge

———

Liberty Needs Glasses

Excuse me but Lady Liberty needs glasses
And so does Mrs. Justice by her side
Both the broads R blind as bats
Stumbling thru the system
Justice bumped into Mutulu and
Trippin' on Geronimo Pratt
But stepped right over Oliver
And his crooked partner Ronnie
Justice stubbed her Big Toe on Mandela
And liberty was misquoted by the Indians
Slavery was a learning phase
Forgotten without a verdict
While Justice is on a rampage
4 endangered surviving Black males
I mean really if anyone really valued life
And cared about the masses
They'd take 'em both 2 Pen Optical
And buy 2 pairs of glasses

———

Hail, Dalibunga!

Hail, Dalibunga! It's Bongani Sitole.
Words of truth have been exposed.
A bull, kicking up dust, displacing stones.
Dust rises, ant heaps are broken.
A man, staring at the sky till the stars tumble down.
I say to you, Dalibunga, I say to you, Madiba,
I've done nothing, people of my home.
I remember you as a man I met at Mfulo in '57.
I say that you and Slovo played hide and seek,
disguising yourselves to conceal your identity,
So you wouldn't be recognised.
You're the light-skinned Paramount of the Thembu,
The son of the Khonjwayo princess,
A king born of the nation's princess,
A bright man of the nation's woman,
Someone who stamped his feet on Umtata Mountain
And the whites took fright,
Someone who drank once from the waters of the sea
Till the water dried up and revealed the stones,
A king who did wonders among various nations,
So the Thembu house was shocked:
Saying, 'What manner of king is this?'
I've done nothing, Thembu, I've done nothing.
One day the Boers set down two bags,
A bag of soil and a bag of cash,
Saying the king should pick the one he liked.
King Sampu's son did a wondrous thing:
Good Lord! He picked the bag of soil, and other chiefs
            took the bag of cash!
I've done nothing, people of my home.
One day I spoke, shocking the Boers with confusion.
They said, 'Who's this hounding us?
What battle's he hounding us to?'
So the whites harassed me,
Made me harassed, just like them,
In my very own land.
Alas, Dalibunga, you're a chief to be nurtured,

Alas, Dalibunga, you're a chief to be guarded,
You surprised me, tall son of Mandela,
You surprised me, lash that whipped certain nations:
In consultations with whites overseas
You terrified whites who never talk to blacks.
I say to you, old man,
I say to you, Madiba of Zondwa,
I've spoken, I'll not speak again,
I say to you be strong, Dalibunga,
Be strong, Madiba, our ancestors watch you,
Our grandmothers promised you'd not die in jail.
Bring change, Madiba, things aren't right.
You were raised, Dalibunga, on Dalindyebo's cows' milk
So you would grow to stand tall
Like the river reeds of this country.
The men of our home shuffled their feet:
Cowards! Your cowardice will be bared!
So says the poet of tradition.
Long live Dalibunga!
Long live this old man!
Long live Sophitshi's Madiba!

(Translated from Xhosa by Russell Kaschula)

———

Nelson

So Mr Mandela, sir, at last
You are 'free': as I read it
You had nothing to do but read
For twenty-six years while you

Made history. But you are free
Do Mr Mandela just this, conquer
With your spirit what we outsiders being
'Free', have lost in the cause of history.

———

Boipatong

In agony and agape
people bite the sky
swallow obfuscating cloud
struggle to disinter sun;
a diet of vapour
and debilitating rain
striving to make light again

Armoured with ignorance
ruddered by hate
demons unleashed
by dividend draculas
who lurk in suburban bunkers
twice removed from stench
of departments
plagued by siege
and revelations
of compulsive greed

One more harvest
yielding grief;
incendiaries the seasons' flowers
capital the manic gardener.
Anguish of Boipatong
an echo of Bulhoek
Sharpeville and Sebokeng;
implanted by blanched executives
lies designed to silence
undermine the slickest tongues.
haunted and muted
they tolerate the bleeding of innocents
but draining nation's veins
is dredging their own
arterial resources

Nameless
faceless
profit fodder
moulds fleets
of mansions and mercs;
shores up serial yachts and
a timeless procession
of precision watches
clock up stocks
and shares
in recreational flutters;
embellished meals
courtesy diner's card
ensures recurring dream
of meat
by overambitious Mvusi
would spit him
on a hostel spear;
longing for a damp-free dwelling
fitted Nkosazana
with new set of body vents
while infant's hunger
for love of mother
planted metal
in her head

History not repeated
but illuminative;
lumpen black hundreds
revive wilted Czar
with Jewish compost;
Benito's blackshirts
administer kiss of life
to Roman corporations
by flaying Gramsci's kin;
Third Reich ovenstokers
feeding Jewish-Bolshevik plot
up chimneys
of Krupp and Farben
with zionist connivance
still denied
despite Sabra and Shatilla;
not to mention
obliteration of
Hanoi and Haiphong
by eyeless birdmen
of Pentagonia
and massacre at My Lai
by LBJ's head-hunting
leathernecks

Track back to future with
Battalion 32 in 92
also Unita
Renamo and Koevoet
to name but three
custodians of economic and
moral monopoly;
cosmopolitan entrepreneurs
will not be deviated
by any partisan
let alone
patriotic consideration
short of golden handshakes
and promises of
season tickets for life
into Sun City
rocking in perpetuity
after all has gone back
(not to the people) but
to more or less normal
with elevation
of flexible black elements
into cost effective zone
of heaven
while blood's still legal tender
in bases ringing Boipatong

Supping at Last Codesa
stale bread and
watered-down wine
while de Klerk
had his cake
and ate it
washed down with
vintage 'Black on Black'
matured in Witdoek's
busy mortuaries

Predictably dubbed
'Judas of the Peace'
by warlord
to overrule
all warlords
we refused to parrot after him
'peace at any price!'
at price of peace

Remembering
more of us
have bitten dust
swirling around
de Klerk's boots
than in all dust storms
put together
since DF Malan decreed
ashes and dust
a national aspiration

Pulling a fast one
but never his punch
this benign crocodile
(some say Gorbachev look-alike)
man of the moment
but not of tomorrow
transnational troubleshooter
and political paramedic
beamed down to Boipatong
to administer ether
where hours earlier
hired steel held sway
over human ideal

But enlightened eyes
shatter illusions
and limits of his fears
de Klerk
and his entourage of dogs
dematerialised
leaving rage irresistible
under Mandela's flying colours

———

Where is the Freedom for Which We Died?

Whenever I dream during these violent times
I meet up with the martyrs for freedom.

I see Steve Biko again,
And Achmad Timol,
and David Webster,
all, all of them murdered by deeds of hatred.

I also see Nelson Mandela,
a man buried alive in prison
who stepped from his tomb still living
and is the Lazarus of our times.

These are the heroes I think of often,
who knock at the doors of our memory,
who travel around our country
talking together as they look about them
like ancestral spirits of the new South Africa.

Going into the home of a drunkard
they see him beating his wife and children.
'Look at that!' says one of the heroes,
'Is this the freedom for which we died?'

Entering a township
they find the skies full of flames
and people running confusedly round the streets
like termites whose home has been kicked over.
'And look at that!' says another of the heroes.
'Is this the freedom for which we died?'

Going into a school
they see the pupils bickering with the teachers
and two boys stabbing each other.
'And look at that!' says another of the heroes.
'Is this the freedom for which we died?'

Walking the city streets at night
they find the homes locked and barred
as if the people had built their own prisons
and lived inside them huddled in fear.
'I can't believe it!' another of them says.
'Is this the freedom for which we died?'

These are the heroes I think of often,
these are the shades of the new South Africa,
and this is the question they ask the living,
'Where is the freedom for which we died?'

(Translated from isiZulu by the poet)

———

Tamed

You come out onto the dais,
distant as a god, a totem, raise
your arms and we roar
with an adoration like a rage.
But the trees are dumb,
the wind stalled, the air
ambivalent as a new wine.
There should be doves
to racket up in a salute,
but even the pigeons,
crouched on their window ledges, ring
us with their stricken rigid wings.
I strive
to tiptoe, to see
you the better, but my blood,
like the wind, has stalled
and I am mired in the flesh
turned slush of my feet as my fists
pump the air and I shout
old slogans old gods
hear as but the cold
seas' mechanical praise.
Beside me, a black
man in glasses, moustache's
white-as-a-milk-
slick waiting to be tongued,
face falling in,
turns to me his back
in its suit of a fine cloth,
frets behind the glasses, hooks
out a single shining tear.
hemming me, two
louts with wet lips, eyes hot
as coals a wind blows
to this side of flame,
still their roistering, stand
imploded and intent,

agelessly beyond their age.
One looks up, around
him, seeing only you,
and his face lights
with something of the sublimity
he must believe you bring,
beneficently will lend.
Your hand cuts,
and it silences us
as though it severed tongues,
and I am looking back to the once
the hand held mine
and it was still the man's
the sourness of the cells
gloved with the sourness of a death,
and your eyes were still those
of one running from the long hell.
And now?
Are you still he that,
stripped to his soul,
denied it its death,
sought the dream in even stone and iron?
A mannikin hands
you the typed sheets of your speech.
You shuffle them, tap
the microphone, gently clear
an old phlegm from your throat –
and are oracle,
measured thunder of your voice
doomsday's in a square.
But then comes
the small fumble of the tongue,
the stretching thin
of the fabric of the spell,
and the words are sad
old slogans that fall
likes stones onto a stone,
and I see now the white,
imperial quiff is blued,
though the eyes

still scuttle in an old skull,
and the mannikin is feeding
you with more words,
stolidly as into a machine,
and a dignitary lifts
a cuff to check a watch,
to covertly signal now
is the time to ring
down the curtain, move
onto a new square in an old game.
You heed.
We rise in rapture, stretch
up our hands to the kitsch,
alienating pedestal we've piled
for your pinioning, and you reach
out to bless
us and I am hanging my head –
amongst these many thousand others
hanging my head lest
you see me weep,
knowing, as I know,
that there is no crying like
the lamentation of old men.

_____

The Long-Distance South African

1

The passage is an axis of hush and gloom running down
the middle of our house. At one end the black bakelite
telephone rests on its ledge; at the other stands the built-
in cupboard, stacked with epochs of clothing and
suitcases, along with mothballs and Cobra floor-polish,
toiletries and tins of anti-termite solution, all ready to
stink sweetly past the open door.

A mangy old settee leans against one side of the passage,
with a seat that humps up where the springs are bust.
Against the other side, a tall iron bookcase rises to the
ceiling, its books squeezed together tight as a trainload of
refugees. Night after night adults pause there with skew
heads, deciphering all the titles.

It is 1960, the year my parents buy the house in
Johannesburg with its goose-pimpled pale green walls
and giant tree whose wood is soft as paper. It is 1961,
1962. Still adults come to the bookcase, stop and hunch
and tip-toe perilously on a kitchen chair, necks bent under
the moulded ceiling. Sometimes they slump with a prize
book on the settee, recovering.

But each year there are fewer of them. Several, I am told,
have skipped the country. I think of the country as a thick
rope, and various adults gaily skipping. I am forced to
revise my ideas sometime later when the newspaper
publishes a photograph of a motor car, in the boot of
which the police brought one of them back from
wherever he had skipped to.

Meanwhile, those survivors who come round are all
sealed into the sitting room with my father. No one is
allowed to open the door onto the passage, where the
smooth-eared telephone waits patiently to pick up any
stray phrases.

My mother is not in there with them. Quite late one
night I see her go treading down the passage in her
slender dressing gown, past the sitting room where
smoke and strategies pile against the door. She is tired
and her features are pale as water, the fire of her glance
doused. She has become a stranger in her own house.

It is 1964 and my father is arrested. He neither dies nor is
he there. His shadow dents the cushions of every chair.
Outside, children dive-bomb swimming pools, dogs barb
the air with their din. History stops where the suburbs
begin.

It is 1965 or 6. My mother buys a set of cups and saucers
and stows them away in the passage cupboard all the
years of my father's sentence. They are her porcelain
dream of leaving, a constant lesson in tenuousness.
Sitting in their dark tissue paper they are forerunners,
waiting for the other objects in the house to join them on
a long-delayed journey to somewhere else.

2

The garden gate is on its last legs. The worn latch hardly
holds; one wooden upright, wobbly with termites, is
lashed to the same fence which it should be saving from
collapse. The ground under the gate has been removed
by stormwater summer after summer till any fat cat could
worm its way through.

But right now there is nothing and no one at the gate.
From the sitting room window the only creature I can see
is a butcher bird, high above the hedge on a telephone
wire, ticking away the seconds with its tail. It is
November 30th, 1973. I watch the gate and wait.

In the garden, the sun drives against drought-ridden
yellow grass, long arched leaves of agapanthi and the
lemon tree that never grew. Yet another car slides under
the plane leaves outside, gets mottled and doesn't stop.
The more I wait, the less he is there. Shadows on the
meat-red porch deepen against the glare.

I turn from the window to the quiet inside. The whole
house has been dusted and waxed till it shines like a bride.
My mother has weighed the kitchen table down with
delicacies for breakfast, fruits and cheeses and hams. It is
nearly lunch-time when I heard the car doors slam.

He advances down the garden path, jacket flapping, arms
half-lifted from his sides as if the earth were a tightrope,
as if it were difficult to cross over, as if after all this time
we would still never reach each other's arms. My father,
and to one side my mother, pale with anxiety and elation.
And behind them the gate, closed against the minions of
the state.

My father, full length for the first time in years, tipped
sleek and alien into our lives, my father whom I have
supplanted, coming to hug me. I am against him, buried in
the good leather and olive smell of his skin. I am with him
under the nectarine tree, his smile is ripe but mine is
aching and green.

He enters by the front door, and the floor tilts under his
hesitant, uneven steps; the walls incline, a brass pestle
tremors in its mortar. He is in the kitchen meeting Jane,
the black woman who has mothered his children all this
time. She knows this is goodbye, but goes on glowing
steadily. We've been given three days in which to pack
up and put to sea.

We sit down to breakfast, and sky purrs at the windows,
already water presses under the floorboards. My father
considers the feast before him, hardly knowing what to
choose. There is no glass across his face, no guard to
snipe at forbidden words, no bug snooping for them as
they fall. We can talk about anything we want, and for
once there is nothing to say at all.

Three days. One brother and one sister return from
school to find a long-waylaid father. Five pairs of curtains
are drawn against prying eyes, and the suburbs disappear
forever. Thousands of books lie down for the first time in
ages. But my father remains upright. I find him motionless
in the passage in the middle of the night, nine years of
absence strapped securely as a parachute to his back.

Three days it takes for the waters to carry us away. They
tear themselves white from the shores of the Cape;
tirelessly they buoy us up on their shoulders. And when
their task is done they retire from the far shore, mooring
us in one more harbour of estrangement as they have
moored generations before.

3

This table did not follow us across the sea. It occupies a
corner of my parents' London kitchen, white and round
and unremarkable on its one leg and three toes, waiting
to accumulate a bit of history. Meanwhile my mother
bends at the nearby oven, slides out a date loaf and
announces that it is time for tea.

The other members of the family come gradually unstuck
from various limpet occupations that have lasted all the
way through Sunday. And before long we are gathered in
the kitchen, where the plump, rectangular date loaf sits
smoking on the table.

Here we are in our new lives, each finding out what it
means to be a foreign body. Here are the cups and saucers
from before, filled with English tea-bag tea. We sit down
and set to, with a pitter of porcelain and steel. The
heating pipes burp intermittently.

Hardly four o'clock and the day fades, pot plants suck
twilight from the window panes. The sky goes toxic
orange above suburban motorways. We finish our tea,
the cake, the crumbs; stack plates away and sit back down
at the half-dark table.

Someone mentions gooseberries, and soon the old house
in Johannesburg comes up. Somewhere in the garden
there was an unassuming bush that gave an annual crop
of little papery lanterns. Press one open and out popped a
tight amber Cape gooseberry, with a whiff of petrol and a
taste of sour honey. But as to the bush's exact location,
we can't seem to agree.

So my father traces the house in the middle of the table,
with a tentative cross for the bush, just behind it, to the
right. Someone adds in the giant tree, the rockery, the
outside room where Jane, our pillar of strength, lay down
at night. Someone else puts up a splitpole fence across
one end of the table, and resolutely replants the
gooseberry bush against it.

One by one our hands record what we remember of the
house and garden, till everything of import is more or
less where it should be. And when finally the wayward
gooseberry bush has been democratically rooted, we lean
back and survey our bonds and our losses.

Darkness fills the kitchen now, our hands rest empty at
the table's edge. The house and garden sink without a
trace. Between us there is nothing but a flat dim disk, an
indecipherable stretch of water in a moonless place.

4

The man comes walking, tall and solemn and slow. One
of his hands bends into a fist, an old fist, tight with
stamina and ash. He raises it before the crowd, which
presses in on him and takes possession of his name.

The man's suit has an executive cut and sheen for the
T.V. cameras that scatter his image across millions of
screens. But the set of his face is answerable to no one,
more resolute as he comes closer, and more remote.

He advances wearily, restraining with his pace the entire
procession of loyal aides and gunslingers, high priests,
kith and kin, praise-singers and hangers-on. It's been
twenty-seven years of bootsteps and breaking stones.
Out of time with all the elation, he is still alone.

There are only a few yards to go now, the ground widens
under his feet. It is February 11th, 1990. History waits for
him like a big smart car and he gets in. The crowd packs
the rear-view mirror and windscreen; the ignition is
switched on. The man is back in the land of the living, his
myth is in contact with oxygen.

One long ocean away I watch it happen. Wind spreads
the chiffon curtains in our flat; the zinc roofs of Paris are
lacquered with rain. I switch channels following the man
to the car again and again.

Then he is gone and another man comes walking. He is
my newly freed father, crossing the garden of absence to
meet me. Above us, a single butcher bird on a telephone
wire. The sun is hot but I can't feel its fire.

I am against him and the ground under our feet changes
to water. We belong to no single place, ours is the history
of those who cross over. And at the docks to wave us
goodbye there are only a few acquaintances and no doubt
a few cops.

Car tyres stick like velcro to the wet streets outside;
windows flicker with the foggy light of T.V. One more
news programme and Mandela comes walking, behind
him the unsealed door of an entire country.

I pick up the phone and call South Africa. Hell, I say, and
the echo of my voice returns to me from under the sea.
Hello, a friend answers. Are you alright? I squeeze the
receiver so hard my hand is white. When a vacuum is
broken, air rushes in. I'm at the far end of the world
listening to the wind.

———

A New Africa

Hail! Nelson!
Hail! Son of Mandela
Will you people all listen
Come closer let's talk
What wrong did we do in this field?
We planted wheat and reap rotten wheat.

Wake up children of peace
Wake up the ship is sinking
Apologise to the Almighty
Yea! Which part of the body is breaking, Madiba?

The ANC roared in 1912
That our forefather's wealth will never end up in the hands
                    of the Whites,
Malan screamed as if Mzilikazi is pinching him,
Marholi roared in jubilation
And said, Malan you cried because you feel the pinch.

Verwoerd took the reigns and things turned more sour,
He told blacks that they are still kids,
Which nation could be led by baboons?
That will happen over my dead body,
As unlearned people I'll give you the book to go and read,
Soon after that there was confusion,
Others started raising their fists
While others raised their hands,
Pandemonium ensued,

Wake up black people do not sleep,
Wake up boys send those cows to the veld,
Africans organized a toyi-toyi to the Parliament,
Under the Table Mountain in 1960,
Rhosana, a school child was flying like a bird,
Saying we are not fighting although this is our country,
Whites responded by saying, your ears are dirty,
Go back, your letter has been written and signed by Verwoerd,
You will get your response in the afternoon at about 6pm,
Soon afterwards there came hippos,
Others suggested escape because death was imminent,
What sort of letter is this one?
A letter written with blood,
Slow thinkers thought this would cause news headlines.

What's wrong Africans?
You the house of Phalo,
Hippos started shooting at Langa township, shaking family halls,
The sound indicated clearly the wrath of the Whites
Yes! The sun set with our heroes that day,
Yes! Lord painful days are no longer scarce,
Mandela screamed at Verwoerd!
Your heat is strong like that of a steam train,
What is black people's real sin unto you?
He disappeared to seek refuge in Lusaka,
We thought he went to the place of safety,
Instead he was preparing for Verwoerd's response.
He came back, Verwoerd said you lad are dirty, and took him to
Robben Island,

Please listen Africans, a big snake is talking at Robben Island,
Die for a good cause and do not live for nothing,
Move away from Verwoerd as he has a rash,
Botha is dishing food he did not cook,
My boys are coming back from Lusaka,
Coming back with vast experience,

Always respect old man's voice,
MK boys came crawling,
Crossing big seas at their backs,
At the head was General Chris Hani,
A brave man from birth,

News travels fast,
Botha turned pale when hearing the news,
And instructed strong operations at the borders,
Instead the heroes gave him a quick answer,
He soon became dizzy and fainted,
He confessed that these boys are clever,
As you are able to read a letter written in isiVambo.

When a lion is in the cul-de-sac it prefers a peace deal,
A slight chance it runs away,
De Klerk came forth and declared peace with Blacks
I am releasing Mandela,
Our big bull came out in 1990,
Fire broke out at Table Mountain,
Firefighters struggled to contain the blaze,
Because the power of God is unbelievable,

Yea! This earth is ever changing,
A leaf never falls away from its mother tree,
Even De Klerk is the same as his brothers,
Instead of giving us freedom, he gave promises,
Promises that are fulfilled by innocent blood.

Makwethu's boys opted for use of force,
Sword for sword,
Mandela shook him and said cool down my brother,
This road is still long,
Let's rest our comrades,
You African legend we are thankful to you,
You were educated at Lusaka and came home with a degree,
This was witnessed by a lucky bird that I saw,
They are fools all those who think ANC will die,
I am referring to you Dalibunga,
Hai! The son of Marholi, you pulled a branch and MK emerged,
That's Madiba, the one who closes African dongas.

My people give me a white beaded bracelet
Because Verwoerd's pain is evident,
People are still complaining even today,
Each home has its fool,
This freedom vehicle must move because people are hungry,
The toyi-toyi must go children of peace,
Pray while you are standing Africans, time is against us,
Forward with struggle Forward!

(Translated from Xhosa by Mandlakayise C. Matyumza.
English version by Morakabe Seakhoa)

Departure from the Isle of Torments
(Mandela's musings)

Soon our silenced syllables will be heard
Because penance for these crimes has come to the end
– this century of wounds born of man's inhumanity –
For in the morn we swept the yard of vengeance clean

And then our third eyes vividly relished the hills of childhood
Avoiding distractions and passions of forgotten trails

Our wading feet were shocked and cleansed by shallow rivers
As we wiped salty memories, suffering the rejuvenating air

Ah! To cross this threshold and tread on new shores
To arrive at the destination of our cherished dream
– beware of the whiplash as our swollen tide breaks –

Despite this past season of torments and sirens
Our arrival at the sacred homestead and ruins of decades
Signals a hasty flight of this vermin that mutilated our limbs

Behold the swaying multitudes, the frenzied laughter:
You did the nation well by returning!

(Translated from isiZulu by Vusi Mchunu)

———

First Election

1

There is a perturbation of spring
grudging the earth.
                                There is
a song of bent branches fighting
the wind. There is a roll of drums

a tumult of voices a thunder

that resonates
                        to stumble
among distant plains and mountains

chinks through
to where he sits, an old man
trapped
in the Cape's wettest months

beside an electric fire,
next to a jabbering television.

Who sits still in a time of joy?

– He remembers a son murdered
                                        along with

the other dead, and their images
flicker in and out of being
like ghosts
                on the evening news

whispering at his ear:

– here is the life I never had,
the life I fought then longed for
these last years

my mouth has stifled within a grave.
Father, all our corpses are forgotten.
The inscriptions on our tombstones

are blurring now: no one
asks if these are our flowers,
no one asks if we might stay.

2

Here's a hard one.

You might fall in love with the Corporation,
but the Corporation can't
much love you back.   (laughter)
Just because

you've got this job today, it doesn't mean
it'll last for ever - the end
of yet another love affair!   (laughter)

Corporations want people
who can benefit them
at this moment:

and just because
you're hip today,
you can't expect that to last:
so what can you do?

– you can learn to market *yourself.*   (applause)

3

Between where children lie and rot
and their fathers sit and lie
are a people
determined to sing, can't sing
stuttering themselves into being
on park benches in shacks
baked by the heat
where few have ever been
                              allowed to rest

who sniff the sky
sense the stirrings of a breeze
in these dragging final seconds
                       of quiescence
before the earth at last
can align again
towards its rain and harvests ...

we await
of our own making

the unexplored languages,
the drums to celebrate
new rhythms across each skin,
our children swinging from
branches groaning with fruit,
the feasts of meat and putu,
the marabous pacing in full dams,
the chittering orbhung nights,
the moans of lovers freed

again every afternoon

our awe
at the gathering cumulus.

Mayibuye!

4

What did we hope,
                    would return?

In a country where we had the temerity
                    to stand up
                    and call ourselves
          reborn
                    they say:

                    NOW IS THE TIME
                                        to switch to Caltex
                    NOW IS THE TIME
                                        to optimise your profile
                    NOW IS THE TIME
                                        for funky dreads
                    NOW IS THE TIME
                                        to find a committee
                                        and sit on it
                    NOW IS THE TIME
                                        for the sly passage
                                        of coin gritting across coin

while policemen bumble about our streets
apologising for the fact
they shoot as straight as ever

we,
     who longed for
a birth that could vindicate
a history in shards like glass
scraped along the palate

are instead offered

this nation, this other
of our trusting, still
feeding off the contents
of its own belly, its bright
semblance caught
in tourists' photographs

we,

      who sought a voice
      to call each face towards

      who longed to find a space

      so the millions who
      have always had to listen
      could not only start to speak
      but eat enough to dream

      one by one
      fumble for each other
      and suspect

             that somewhere
      in this glimmering dawnscape

the plump stars of the old moon
are rolling in the dough.

5

You must learn to bury the past.

*The only paradigms that fit
are the ones that fit today.*

*Employees and employers
should no longer see
themselves in competition.*

You have to develop a –
how should I put this? –
a synergy
yes, a synergy
between yourselves as workers,
between yes your new boss
and you, to develop

a better life for all,
for all of us amongst you.

6

All the rapt racial faces cloned from mineral water
in seance at last with the Cellphone God
mumbling rote paeans to the Asian Miracle
or scrabbling towards every unreachable
vista of fashion

– the leguaan said to the polecat,
it's been nice meeting you,
it's nice and sunny here:
I like it on the river bank, now you
must come and play
with me in my water.

The polecat listened.
It jumped right in. Ah!
You know what?
The leguaan it was fine;
the polecat came out rotten wet
and stinking!

            eager to learn
from the World Bank and Development Donors
and other consultants on despair
how to be fishers of men
till Africa heaves,

a fish hooked on the end of the line
a mask termited to the point of implosion
a virgin smirking from promise of new knowledge

(for those who submit
to the malarial twitchings of power

there will always be

delightful guests to feast on
museums that cannot tell the truth
and fresh blood on the altar).

7

For you who long to live the land,
a field of stones to plough –

for you who cherish sight,
the dark rind of a candle –

for you who pine for gentleness,
the kiss of spooks on celluloid –

for those who wish to see,
a mine-shaft's vantage point.

8

You see, Mandela, what does he say?
He says we must all study.
I don't criticize him –
that we must all study –
we can all sing, but
we can't all talk.

You see, those who studied
we were helping them,
us in the struggle.
If we all went to school
who would cause havoc
with the Boers?
Would Mandela be out of jail?

Some of us are old already.
I'm 28 years old. What
am I going to do at school
when I'm this old, tell me?
You find a white kid who
is 21, 22 having a car
along with those on the gravy.
A Sprinter, whatever, BMW
a two-door. They have
their own car and I
never had a car. My father
never had a car.

You see,
thieves are a result
of things like that.

9

Give us back our land!

the country of our labour,
a place where we can doubt

> – I tell you

here where we stand
we mean to stand.

———

Who Dun It?

Soldiers unite
De war is over
Now people have fe talk
An get fe know each other
Exiles flying home like birds going south
Because Mandela is in an apartheid is out,
Day dream a multiracial dream
Day see de grim reality
Recall dat hand dat waz unseen
Before de people victory,
Dere is much work dat must be done
No sense in living in de past
Still dere's smoke comin from de gun
So there are questions I muss ask
But,
Nobody done apartheid
Day were all revolutionaries.

Nobody took de land an divided de people
Dere waz no reason to build townships
Cause nobody done no evil,
Nobody introduce a state of emergency
Nobody did anything so no one is guilty,
Nobody banned de books
No one set up road blocks
Everybody waz supporting de Communists and Blacks
Everybody knew apartheid put in practice would not work
Yes, everybody waz protecting de Blacks from getting hurt,
Yes,
Nobody done apartheid
Day were all revolutionaries.

Dere were no
Black hotels   White hotels
Black music   White music
And if dere waz, all hated it
An everyone waz fighting it,

No
Black parks   White parks
Black trains   White trains
Black land   White land
An other land fe Indians

Nobody killed Steve Biko
No
Dere were no Pass Laws
Day were all at Soweto
Fighting fe de cause,
Nobody watch Sophiatown burn
No ting waz in de banks
Nobody haz a lesson to learn
No one voted in de tanks,
Dat's right,
Nobody done apartheid
Day were all revolutionaries.
So no one want revenge
An dere's no one to avenge
De boycotts an de protests were not needed,
All muss now pretend dere's no past
An become friends
An juss sey tings like
Common sense succeeded.

Now a moments silence
For dem dat could not stay.

An a moment of nonviolence
For dem dat passed away,

Yet more moments to remember
De times yu muss forget
Why go to Australia?
Dere's nothing to regret
Because,
Nobody done apartheid
Day were all revolutionaries.

I'd juss like fe know
How a hater thought
An how it waz to play around
At segregated sport,
I'd juss like fe know
How day will cope wid words like
Share,
An how it waz day slept at night,
When death waz everywhere,
I'd juss like fe know
What made dem tick and tock
An what's it like to be on top
Den find yu have to stop,
I'd juss like fe know
What day think of those next door
An if day still believe de land is theirs
For evermore,
But,
Nobody done apartheid
Day were all revolutionaries.

―

South Africa: Memorial Wall

*Written after the signing of the new constitutional accord, and to
praise all those who gave their lives for democracy in South Africa*

Is any price too high for peace?
The dead heroes gone to earth
still hold their ground.

Rick Turner, the just man
who passed through the eye
of the needle, shot down.

David Webster, last seen elate
weaving in a dance with his brothers.
He lies in a pool of blood at his gate.

Steve Biko, the rational leader
in chains, tortured in a cold cell.
Blood and pain surround his wounded head.

Helen Joseph, her tall proud spine
as she led that giant chanting swag
of women to Pretoria, arrested by time.

Jeremy Cronin, the people's tongue in jail,
his wife doubly absented by death,
soldered by suffering to the black soul.

Ruth First, foremost in courage,
her life a gift to the future
exploding in her face.

Mandela our mandala
of hope and peace
so long a prince in hiding
let out like a shout.

All the dusty desolate townships of death:
black flesh hacked, tyres afire,
hooded men with guns in trains.

All of the weeping women
waiting for their dead to return
to matchbox houses in Soweto.

No more laughing children carrying water.

All of the heroes
who seeded this harvest
deep under ground.
May they shine like suns on the new day:
Biko   Sisulu   Tambo   Mandela.

Longlive!   Longlive!   Longlive!

———

Killing Memory

For Nelson and Winnie Mandela

the soul and fire of windsongs must not be neutral
cannot be void of birth and dying
wasted life
locked
in the path of vicious horrors
masquerading
as progress and spheres of influence

what of mothers
without milk of willing love,
of fathers
whose eyes and vision
have been separated from feelings of earth and growth,
of children
whose thoughts dwell
on rest and food and
human kindness?

Tomorrow's future rains in
atrocious mediocrity and suffering deaths.

in america's america the excitement is over
a rock singer's glove and burning hair
as serious combat rages over
prayer in schools,
the best diet plan,
and women
learning how to lift weights
to the rhythms of
"what's love got to do with it?"

ask the children,
always the children caught in the
absent spaces of adult juvenility
all
breakdancing and singing to
"everything is everything" while
noise occupies the mind as
garbage feeds the brain.

in el salvador mothers search for their sons
and teach their daughters the way of the knife.

in south afrika mothers bury hearts without bodies
while pursuing the secrets of forgotten foreparents.

in afghanistan mothers claim bones and teeth from
mass graves and curse the silent world.

in lebanon the sons and daughters receive horror hourly
sacrificing childhood for the promise of land.

in ethiopia mothers separate wheat from the desert's dust
while the bones of their children cut through dried skin.

tomorrow's future
may not belong to the people,
may not belong to dance or music
where
getting physical is not an exercise but
simply translates into people working,
people fighting,
people enduring insults and smiles,
enduring crippling histories and black pocket politics
wrapped in diseased blankets
bearing AIDS markings in white,
destined for victims that do not question
gifts from strangers
do not question
love of enemy.
who owns the earth?

most certainly not the people,
not the hands that work the waterways,
nor the backs bending in the sun,
nor the boned fingers soldering transistors,
not the legs walking the massive fields,
nor the knees glued to pews of storefront or granite churches
nor the eyes blinded by computer terminals,
not the bloated bellies on toothpick legs
all victims of decisions
made at the Washington monument and lenin's tomb
by aged actors viewing
red dawn and the return of rambo part IX.

tomorrow
may not belong to the
women and men laboring,
hustling,
determined to avoid contributing
to the wealth
of gravediggers from foreign soil
& soul.
determined to stop the erosion
of indigenous music
of building values
of traditions.

memory is only precious if
you have it.

memory is only functional
if it works for you.
people
of colors and voices
are locked in multibasement state buildings
stealing memories
more efficient
than vultures tearing flesh
from
decaying bodies.

the order is that the people are to
believe and believe
questioning or contemplating
the direction of the weather is
unpatriotic.

it is not that we distrust poets and politicians.

we fear the disintegration of thought,
we fear the cheapening of language,
we fear the history of victims and the loss of vision,
we fear writers whose answer to
maggots drinking from the open
wounds of babies
is
to cry genocide while demanding
ten cents per word and
university chairs.
we fear politicians
that sell coffins at a discount
and consider ideas of blasphemy
as young people world over bleed from the teeth while
aligning themselves with whoever
brings the food.
whoever brings the love.

who speaks the language of
bright memory?

who speaks the language of
necessary memory?

the face of poetry must be fire erupting volcanoes,
hot silk forging new histories,
poetry delivering light greater than barricades of silence,
poetry dancing, preparing seers, warriors, healers
and parents beyond the age of babies,
poetry delivering melodies that cure dumbness & stupidity
yes, poets uttering to the intellect and spirit,
screaming to the genes and environments
revitalizing the primacy of the word and world.
poets must speak the language of the rain,

decipher the message of the sun,
play the rhythms of the earth,
demand the cleaning of the atmosphere,
carry the will and way of the word,
feel the heart and questions of the people
and be conditioned and ready
to move.

to come
at midnight or noon

to run against the monied hurricane in this
the hour of forgotten selves,
forgiven promises
and
frightening whispers
of rulers in heat.

_____

Haiku

The world listens
when Nelson Mandela talks.
His dream gives us hope.

(Translated from Dutch)

——

Causality and Chance in Love

Chapter 1

His parents
and my parents
caused it all.

That's not true. God, laughing as he turned the page.

Two atoms coughed out
by time's collapsing star.

Libra ascending straight into Scorpio
through Sharpeville, Robben Island and Mowbray.
Arriving in Sea Point
when the law was repealed.

Now we are possible.
Necessary and sufficient conditions.

This happy world that fills our arms.

Chapter 2

Robben Island was more useful
than the little Swiss chalet
with the man and the lady
swinging in and out unreliably
or stuck; the mercury still as a dead ant.

IF YOU SEE   IT WILL BE

the clear outline of the island   rain is on the way, and winter winds
a smudge of land in a brown haze   there is dangerous smog in the air
a shimmering blue blur   there will be long and windless heat

'The healthy colony of penguins
is Robben Island's pride and joy.'

'I remember the first time all of us heard children's voices in the quarry. It was as though we had suddenly been struck by lightning. We all stood dead still, and every one of us was waiting for the moment when we would glimpse that child. And of course it wasn't allowed. The warders quickly went and made sure that we didn't actually see the kids. Just those lone voices – the one occasion in ten years that I actually heard the voice of a child.'

Chapter 3

Mist rising on the winter waves
swathed your quarried words in veils
and blew them in to fill my chest with sleeplessness.

I watched the kelp arms of sea creatures reaching through the swell.
You caught the glint of closed windows on the sunlit hills.

Only the wind passing across your lips
and then across my lips, preoccupied with its cargo of rain,
could have imagined us both in the same breath.

Chapter 4

We two waltzing strangely across sand bearing us
tideward, looking over each other's shoulders

at our futures, their lightless eternities
radiating power. Space is curved. We will meet each other
again and again in our pasts that call themselves home,
a little distance from the sunset come to fetch us.

This laughing history that fills our arms.

———

Macbeth

Last week my son, Ben, rang from South Africa,
wanted a recipe for cinnamon cake.
'Just put the two mixtures in anyhow,' I said,

'they always run together as it cooks'.
Tonight he rings again from the theatre –
it's Macbeth in Zulu and he doesn't know the plot.

I remember the fifteen-year-olds struggling
with Shakespeare. Then it was Macbeth,
Scotland's striker, wanting to be manager,

bumped off Duncan, ran the team himself,
couldn't keep his best players, sacked
Banquo: Macduff resigned, joined England.

Neither Macbeth nor his wife could get
a proper night's sleep after that.
His wife died and Macbeth found he'd scored

nothing but own goals, the last one thinking
he was a match for Macduff. Macbeth lost
Scotland and his head. Duncan's son took over....

'Well, there's this fellow Buthulezi, O.K?
ambitious sort of bloke, envies Mandela',
I say, desperate to squash a five-act play

and the whole of South Africa into a long-
distance telephone call. 'Got the picture,'
says Ben, 'cheers, it's about to start.'

―――

If I Woz a Tap-Natch Poet

'dub poetry has been described as ... "over-compensation
for deprivation"'
Oxford Companion to Twentieth Century Poetry

'mostofthestraighteningisinthetongue'
Bongo Jerry

if I woz a tap-natch poet
like Chris Okigbo
Derek Walcot
ar T.S. Eliot

I woodah write a poem
soh dym deep
dat it bittah-sweet
like a precious
memari
whe mek yu weep
whe mek yu feel incomplete

like wen yu lovah leave
an dow defeat yu kanseed
still yu beg an yu plead
till yu win a repreve
an yu ready fi rack steady
but di muzik done aready

still inna di meantime
wid mi riddim
wid me rime
wid mi ruff base line
wid me own sense a time

goon poet haffi step in line
caw Bootahlazy mite a gat a couple touzan
but Mandela fi him
touzans a touzans a touzans a touzans

if I woz a tap-natch poet
like Kamau Brathwaite
Martin Carter
Jayne Cortez ar Amiri Baraka

I woodah write a poem
so rude
an rootsy
an subversive
dat it mek di goon poet
tun white wid envy

like a candhumble/voodoo/kumina chant
a ole time calypso ar a slave song
dat get ban
but fram granny

                    rite
                    dung
                    to
                    gran
                    pickney
each an evry wan
can recite dat-deh wan

still
inna di meantime
wid mi riddim
wid mi rime
wid mi ruff base line
wid mi own sense a time

goon poet haffi step in line
caw Bootahlazy mite a gat couple touzan
but Mandela fi him
touzans a touzans a touzans a touzans

I woodah write a poem
soh beautiful dat it simple like a plain girl
wid good brains
an nice ways
wid a sexy dispozishan
an plenty compahshan
wid a sweet smile
an a suttle style

still
mi naw goh bow an scrape
an gwaan like a ape
peddlin noh puerile parchment af etnicity
wid ongle a vaig fleeting hint af hawtenticity
like a black Lance Percival in reverse
ar even worse
a babblin bafoon whe looze im tongue

no sah
nat atall
mi gat mi riddim
mi gat mi rime
mi gat mi ruff base line
mi gat mi own sense a time

goon poet bettah step in line
caw Boothalazy mite a gat couple touzan
but Mandela fi him
touzans a touzans a touzans a touzans

———

from **Ogoni**

VI. before history we stand

(*'this mandela man must be careful with his unguarded statements or
else we african leaders will deal with him with alacrity!!!'*)

lily-livered counterfeit leaders go hailing their big-booted
brothers' dark deeds
thugs must protect thugs
a dog's friends must be dogs and eat filth
dictators cannot but shield their shadowy sibling
the lion must lord it over the cowered lambs depending on its largesse
black africa's flying elephant must enjoy trampling on the grass
under its feet
so mandela calls for sanctions and sanity
while
his mad critics call for caution and brotherly support
africa their africa is nobody's colony
africans their africans are no longer slaves
africa their africa must decide its own destiny
africans their africans can solve their own problems
with murder
with mayhem
with manipulation of the poor people become their property

meanwhile
civilised society has expressed its shock
it has condemned the criminals with words of
wisdom
while waiting and watching and washing its hands
unclean

after blowing hot
the great western front's now almost cold and quiet
after breathing fire and threatening hell
after promising everything and doing nothing
as usual

243

as before history we stand
some are wondering and waiting for what the great west would do
the great west in its almighty wisdom
as if africa were america
as if burundi would ever be bosnia
as if rwanda would ever be russia
as if exile would ever be home

(*'mandela is our man o! a true african leader who is now ready to cooperate with us!'*)

———

Invisible Ink

Watching our quiet affronted neighbour
slap loud white paint across obscenities
scrawled on his backyard gate,
I imagine all those unseen silent figures,
their spraycan shadows shouting
from walls, bridge-spans, old garage doors.

There's something I admire about them,
though I've never ventured further
than a scratched desk top myself
and once was made to eat
the whole page of invective
I'd scribbled through an R.I. lesson.
But it's never been for me,
hanging upside down from a motorway bridge
to write Tories Out or Free Mandela.

I stay at home, silent and unseen,
and as you turn your back
to read the Sunday paper
or reach to put your cup down on the floor,
my finger traces words across your skin
I'd never dare say to your face.

———

Evidence of Ancestry

1

My eager pick
attacks rock,
shards and sparks
and whizz of shrapnel
zap at specs.
An acrid whiff
like cordite
fleetingly teases.
Petrified sediments
flake and fragment
reveal bony filigree.
Its ivory deceptively organic
silicon usurper
a virtual reality.

Awe open-ended
I gently chip and brush
juggle dust with gravel.
Emerging quadruped
almost familiar
like "all God's creatures"
but essentially infidel.
A reptilian-mammalian transitional
so-called Diictodon
or two-tusker
most common denizen
grazing Gondwanaland
progenitor Karoo mutton
easy meat
off the bone
consolidated as stone.

Withering under an indifferent sun
my wintered hide
craving shade
(maybe a target for melanoma
or cold-blooded adder)
grows scales and fangs
crouching
over my kill.

2

Once prostrate
against
the foothills
of tyrannical peaks
(dwarfing the Drakensberg)
ancient plains
wounded by rivers
and the whiplash of floods
resisted till the uprising
of Antarctica, Andes
and a great piece of the East
at much less than a snailspace
redefined its outline
into Africa.

Once in a million
fossilisation
underwent the elements and
later invasions and depredations.
Endemic apartheid
insisted
ad nauseam
on the illegitimacy
of all organisms
preceding Eden
pinning Broom, Dart and Tobias
under glass with other exotica.
Fossil fuel
of course
one exception to their rule.

3

We seek
it seems
evidence of ancestry
not only
to certify birthright
or to reinforce hegemony
but to know ourselves
as an ingredient of history.

It runs deeper
than national identity
or even
the quests and queries
of anthropology,

but to leap
from two-tusker
to two-fister
needs neither
flight of imagination
nor cool equation
only the flying of time.

4

Now
(in the year of Mandela's abdication)
on a shelf
at home in Clovelly
within sight of
Peer's Cave
and Fish Hoek man
presides an upper jaw bone
of the mother of all mammals
and me.

To Nelson Mandela: A Tribute

That straight walk from the
prison to the gate –
that walk the world saw, and
which changed the world –
it led you through to life from
life withheld,
from broken stones with your
unbroken heart.

To life which you imagined
and then lived,
which once we shared in your
imagining
but soon shared in the
present that you shaped:
the life which gave each
human hope its chance
of turning into truth and
staying true;
the life which understood
what changing takes;
the life which showed us we
become ourselves
in part by watching you
becoming you.

———

Mandela Dead and Alive

Carcere duro ... Delenda apartheid:

I
... I write these pages loose
I forget the trifles
of word and syllable
My pagan faith
feeds my poem
with savage prayers
and animist ritual
To the living tree I say
lend me your roots
plunged deep in the soil
to divide the winds
at this hour of squall
To the naked rock I say
lend me the insolence
enclosed in the immovable
this forge in action
whose fire I need
I ask the mighty tempests
to besiege my bones
to irrigate my throat
My most urgent mission
is to hail Mandela
before any other mass is said...

II

...Mandela I hail your name
Mandela Soundjata
Mandela Nat Turner
Mandela Anne Zinga
Mandela Mackandal
Mandela Golgotha
Mandela Mahatma
Mandela L'Ouverture
Mandela Malcolm X
Mandela Chaka Chaka
Mandela Hammerskjöld
Mandela Luther King
Mandela Guevara
Mandela Feraoun
Mandela Amilcar
Mandela Treblinka
Mandela Palestine
Mandela Luthuli
Mandela Lumumba
Mandela Warsaw
Mandela Santiago
Mandela Samora
Mandela Hiroshima
Mandela Biko
Mandela and all the rest...

III

…XXth Century Parsifal:
the prisoner expires
his quest slung over his shoulder
tired of trying to quench
the fires of hatred
the refusal to take his
well offered black hand
Parsifal-Mandela
no more counts the years
of his soiled Grail
of padlocked words
of paralysed love
of knotted run-up
of slaughtered future
useless Parsifal
illusive Lancelot
the Table is but an isle
Robben the Prison
where Galahad is greying
where dawn turns to thunder
the black hand to a clenched fist
hideous corruption of a heart
changed into a powder keg…

IV

...ships berth no more
to load the old cargo
the indelible leprosy
stigmata branded forever
on the face of History
But History just doesn't care
Ships berth no more
and the weather is at its worst
a whole people incarcerated
in its own home
their only song the cry
of a dirt-cheap death
while birds of the third millennium
are singing in space
I am asked to forget
the cargo of long ago
and to write in the vivid silk
of a planetary era
while the dust thickens
weaving a shroud
for every new body butchered
in the black south of Africa...

V

…me and my vain ink
I feel guilty of writing
only scraps of eternity
my island and its journey
sea-clad woman
her womb and my roots
the open town of my dream
the reading of the undertow
when salt turns to diamond
only to heal the rainbow's wounds
Ah! the difficult death
of one's own solitude.
Within me a whole crowd
intoning thunder
whose lightning I bear
If tomorrow only belongs
to the children of wrath
I must then trample and crush words
pressing vile wine
and let death lurch along
in the black south of Africa…

VI

...I most urgently summon
the masters of the word
those who carry the Earth
in their naked luggage
those who know that Paradise
has neither roof nor doors
and that a single man's rights
denied condemns all Edens
I most urgently summon
all lyrical criers
all word-sharpeners
to cancel Hades
the quadrature of ash
To hell with derision
only the Word creates
only the Word saves
it is never fragile
when it comes to sack death
With detonating larynx
we shall repeat the name
of the man from Rivonia
a sun in quarantine
deadlier than death itself...

VII

…Mandela dead and alive
only the game remains
and it's Aunt Sally
hatred is carnivorous
amidst diamond merchants
who only speculate
One more victim
just news in brief
the show goes on
Mandela is going to die
before he breathes again
the streets' free air
After all these years
no child from the Cape
shall take him by the hand
and recognising the Old Man
leaning against a tree
flesh against plant
that caress so vital
to know he is alive
Mandela dead and alive
a full sun voice
bolted by silence…

VIII

...a bird of worst omen
makes up ploys
in slumber square
and we sleep quietly
lulled by the music
of a well disguised misfortune
the Cape is so far
and our Good Hope
itself so vulnerable
A bird of worst omen
flying plunges us
into the heart of our mirrors
with only our image
for sole resemblance
And Soweto persists
while our little acnes
our bits of misfortune
our delicious bruises
can't wait
Millions set on fire
in one man's destiny
we promise we swear
we shall put it out later...

IX

...later is the alibi
now is the crime
later is oratory
now is real life
What tsetse kiss
has cocooned us so
in deleterious dreams
Thunder is creeping
down to the roots
to knock down
the totem Man
in the black south of Africa
Let us pass through the mirrors
and so touch him on the shoulder
at the exact spot where
widens the smut of solitude
on this corn ensiled
in a most proscribed place
so that never never may rise
whole and good
the promise of a people
healed now from the sacrilege
of bowing and scraping
Let us pass through the mirrors
till we touch Nelson's shoulder...

Epilogue:

    Mandela is alive
    alive and free at last.
    Mandela bears no grudge
    his words weigh no bitterness
    his hand is wide opened
    The first day I met him
    his bonjour was a smile
    his message translated from the soul
    One day – in years to come –
    blue jacaranda raining
    I much hope to put my step in his
    and in unbroken eloquent silence
    listen along a long long way
    to the unique and untold saga
    of Mandela conquistador of freedom.

(Translated from French by Norman Strike)

———

Angels and Oracles

I have poets.
> – Monica Rorvik

No hooting please. Chickens resting.
> – Sign on N3 north of Durban

On bloody acts
that make less human
mankind's brighter sun,
let revulsion rise.
Eclipse the moon's
black evil: so that

innocence and the child
shall reign
so that we may dream
good dreams again
> – Hone Tuwhare, 'O Africa' (June 1960)

The boat is called *Akuna Matata* and it is full of poets. When the moon casts off their festival begins on a bridge of silver over the dark ocean. For eight days their hearts drive the city's taxi vans in a frenzy of toots and whistles. Each one is the name of its articulate lion.

Lord, Lord, Lord Chicken Run Sam the Man

Mr Sheik is the concierge of the Tropicana. He has worked 47 years here and will see there is a good car for bad roads in the mountains. The gentleman intends a longer stay next time he says what do you have?

Feel Good Smoky Joe Revelation

The grandson of Isaiah Shembe looks over at the hillside where a star that fell to earth is laid out in white stones. We have seen angels he says they are among us but in human form.

Wicked Frenzy Fantasy

Someone is stalked and robbed of his wages by six assailants. He is
forced to drink corrosive cleaning fluid that kills him fourteen hours
later.

Pretty Marina Judgement Day Imagination

The grandson of John Langalibalele Dube stands where Gandhi's
house has been rebuilt after fire destroyed part of the Phoenix
Settlement. I become emotional here he says where Gandhi organised
the first satyagraha.

Defiance Classic Just Another Crazy

6.30 pm. Someone is held up at knifepoint two blocks from the hotel.
At 11 Security advises against walking alone or in pairs. Fives and
sixes maybe or sixes and sevens.

Hard Man Seductive Sixteen Bunny Chow

Exequiel Mabote printmaker pulls a prayer meeting out of his drawer
and explains that the angels are coming down close to hear the
confessions of those who also wear white robes and caps.

Tiffany Tycoon Turbo Tours

4.30 am. Someone is shot and killed outside the hotel. The breakfast
cook is upset and we recall hearing shouts and getting up to shut the
window and turn on the air-conditioning.

Snoopy Banana Boy Nemesis Incorporated

Here comes Isaiah Mhlangu with a prophet's mane an angel's smile
and beaded sandals to die for. He's in Community Development. I'm
your driver he says I have my orders but they don't come from God.

Melon Man   Take the A Train   Everything Dingo Touches Stays Gold

At the BAT Centre crouched, aerodynamic wind streaming over folded wings and leopard leotard, a carved angel faces into the divine slipstream wearing dark glasses.

Dinky Diva   King Pleasure   Imagination (2)

Zolani Mkiva is Mandela's praise poet. He wears red robes and a crown of porcupine quills from Zimbabwe. Trouble won't sit on me he says gunning the 4WD with plates that say POET. Among the praise singers who perform at the opening of the cultural centre only the woman has no costume. She is critical and will not be named in the programme or invited to join the group photo. Everyone else holds a certificate and a wooden carving of Africa.

Shady Lady   Ministry of Truth   Love Hotel

Comrade Jesus is a special friend of the executive mayor. Joy Eternity Salvation Unity and Strength also figure as Christ Risen Over Satanic Strategies. He hates the coloniser and will see that justice is done in the new order. He walks without fear in his electorate and there are no bullets in him.

Late in the Day   Hootchy Kootchy   Amandla

Smoking and drinking and drumming in the morning under the Rhino Horn alongside the Hippo Pools. The sun is coming up on the right the moon is going down on the left. *Strawberries / Love tastes like strawberries.* The mountains are bare.

Durban Drakensberg Great Kei River. 28 April - 5 May 2002

———

Fratres (Taking You With Me)

I paint the low hill until I admit
to how the light is on it.
Morning's coldest – working in thermals
and fleeces and socks in triplicate –
a lugworm, bundled bait
for the sky with the thunder-grey roe.

How is the light on the low hill now?
Blood through skin.
Once or twice a day sun opens the vein and
white is white of seagulls – sour Messiahs!
– then another two hundred
of Tommy's rainstained fleeces.

—

I said to Tommy (shifting stone)
whatcha doing and he said
playing at Nelson Mandela
what does it look like?

—

The layby's up for it, grips
your car, windows mossed with thin damp.
Headlamps chuck out sticky webs to slide
from the windscreen and your black/bright forehead.
Headlamps – grasses giant
and shrinking - and us knotted in the hill's hair.

Now you turn the key and the gate's sudden
red iron – the last moment we've netted.
You've picked a soundtrack, you want
to say to keep it light, don't get attached
('no angel') and I want to shock you agreeing
yeh keep it light
and I can carry you a while. For a day or two
I'll have this cumulus bruise (your passing weather)
on my lower lip.

—

Up here it turns out it's less simple
a ewe's fleece
stained by the season of her last tup.

———

The Many Faces of Whitey

I

He wears a round straw hat on his shaven head
Black track suit
On the back: Up the Bucs
Buys 2 litre bottles of Castle
Drinks them in taxis
Swears about the larneys who want to keep the masses out of Sandton
Clips on a Rasta Afrika broach
Likes to boogie to the saxophone
Knows how to break a pipe
When the wind howls on the Cape Flats
Knows how to stir pap till it's smooth and thick
When rain flattens shacks in Diepsloot

2

He carries two cellphones and five bank cards
can't take his eye off the punkies whose black braids
turn Thembi into Priscilla and Thandi into Jane
can't take his hands off their bums and breasts
drinks at a shebeen in Fordsburg
eats hot curry
drinks at a shebeen in Meadowlands
passes out after a twelve hour session
car hijacked at a robot in Doornfontein
tsotsis take his platform shoes and leather jacket
he applies for a job at the Ministry of Communication
writes a tv script about Kandar the African prince
who takes back the People's Land

3

He smokes Winston
plays marabaraba and the Lotto
calls every man bra
wears black shades
reads the Sowetan and Business Day
buys a ticket to Luanda but doesn't fly
buys a ticket to London
comes back from London
forms an Empowerment company
buys a house next to a cabinet minister
becomes a financial advisor to the ruling party
has dinner with Madiba
drinks Johnny Walker with Allan Boesak
is present when Steve Cohen
shits on stage and calls that: art
gets married to a pale woman
with a drug problem

4

He develops a drug problem
buys up old blocks of flats in Hillbrow
becomes a brothel keeper
steals a gun
bribes the cops
learns to play the guitar maskanda style
runs a nightclub in Rockey Street
buys a holiday flat in Uvongo
becomes a dj at YFM
goes to raves disguised as a gymmer
drinks at Kippies
phones in to Radio Metro and bitches about kwerekwere
phones in to the Tim Modise show and slams Hansie Cronje
runs for president of the Young Black Achiever Club and loses
runs for chairperson of Old Eds Health and Racquet Club and wins
sends his step-daughter to a private school in Pretoria
dances with Adelaide Tambo at De Klerk's third wedding
to a Vietnamese ballet dancer
writes a novel about his experiences in exile
falls asleep during a Bafana Bafana semi-final against Togo
is threatened with deportation by Comrade Mbeki
for mispronouncing the word 'renaissance'

5

He is buried on a sunny Sunday morning
his funeral more organised than Joe Slovo's
more powerful than Chris Hani's
sadder than his mother's and father's

rest in peace: Whitey

———

Confessions at Noon 2

'I do not want to go on being a root in the dark,
hesitating, stretched out, shivering with dreams,
downwards, in the wet tripe of the earth,
soaking it up and thinking, eating every day.'
Pablo Neruda

…..I want to be the shoot
the sword of sunlight,
protruding, slicing, piercing
through the air of time
with the hilt of dawn.

I want to live these dreams,
to clasp the moon in my bosom
to soar beyond stars,
to glow, to grow,
to touch and be touched
by lightning's many fingers.

I want to meditate the photosynthetic miracle
in the womb of shriveled leaves,
feeding the skeins and veins
with morsels of fertility.

I want to be the shoot,
hard with scars of gales,
dripping with the rain's seasonal promises
burdened with regurgitated harvests.

I want to be the shoot;
the sword in the hand of Shaka,
the defiance in the gut of Mandela,
sticking out in the face of seasons,
living its dream.

———

When Mandela Goes

When you go chosen soldier in the crusade of dreams
our tears shall not cloud your journey home
we shall receive regret with the tears of triumph
recall yesterday's summons to distant and strange lands
revive heroic cries in the white quarry of cruel islands
where initiation ceremonies marked farewell to lethargy
where oaths were taken as dusk and conscience stood witness
where blood was spilt to curb the bad omen of untimely loss
when love for this land saw stars vanish in the fullness of
uncertain nights
and your wisdom prevailed over the tumultuous inferno of our rage.

When you go Madiba your nobility shall be our lasting inheritance
this land you so love shall continue to love
we shall trail the long and majestic walk
your gallant walk shall be our cross and shepherd.

―――

New Year in Cape Town

It is hogmanay and holidaymakers head back to the city
from beaches at Muizenberg, St James and Noordhoek bay.
In the evening beneath Table Mountain we gather
in Kirstenbosch Gardens, where we sit in the amphitheatre
of a sloping lawn enclosed by trees and aloes to hear
the Cape Town Philharmonic, and Yvonne Chaka Chaka
sings Motherland. Thousands of hand held candles light
the cooling darkness at midnight.

Here they are singing Auld Lang Syne with a zed in the syne.
Nobody seems to know of Robert Burns. And a new year comes
hot on the heels of midsummer. Orion is upside down in the sky.
We have moved beyond dreams and this rainbow nation
dances to salsa music on the lawn; the wind of change
is balmy and strong enough to make candles flicker.
In another part of town the police appeal to the public
to not carry guns at parties.

Soon Tweede Nuwe Jaar will mark the one day of the year
when slaves could walk free from their labour. The minstrel bands
will play through city streets, where stalls advertise Halal Boerewors,
where security fences separate performer from spectator;
as commerce divides participant from consumer the world over;
(in Edinburgh Hogmanay was cancelled – the Cape Times reports –
                  a man
is in trouble for getting too chummy with sharks) as cameras turn
                  celebration
into mass entertainment and tv ratings.

In the museums people are claiming their own space
in history; they are talking about restitution, planning
to rebuild the streets of District Six that were cleared
in the name of apartheid. In community projects they are
photographing poverty, bodymapping AIDS.
And you wonder at times when you drive
past Khayelitsha township and the squatter camps,
what kind of flame is burning there?

Beyond the words of tour guides (free to speak
of their captivity at the visitor centre on Robben Island)
those who continue to struggle are counselled
to 'Carry it lightly'. Reconciliation
is for the generous hearted. Justice is for the full bellied.
And truth is for those who lived through the night in dread
of police raid and torture cell. But how many daughters and sons
are happy to live by their parents' bond?

I remember the television images of Mandela walking free,
and the crowds queuing to vote in 1994. I recall
the Sharpeville Six, and the words of Mandela
imprisoned, the songs of Hamish Henderson,
and the slogans of the ANC. I marched among thirty thousand
to Glasgow Green. I remember the promises we made singing
the words of the Freedom Charter. Forward we will march
to the People's Government.

There is a song to keep singing, for the freedom fighters
who are building communities, educating the children, healing
the sick. Freedom is coming.

———

from **History is the Home Address**

Robben Island: between you and the sea
I stand near the cannon pointing into the sea
I hear it go off in my imagination
and think of the smithereens which fly from its explosion
shattering
disintegrating men
women and children devastated
because there has been Robben Island
here
I walk close to the penguins for the first time
here
I sense a very cold wet hot weather
here
thorny bushes and dry plants
spread and sprawl the dry harsh earth
here
on Robben Island the earth is rocky
and rugged
here dust clings to the leaves and stones
it clings to the walls which
I wish could speak
for I wonder what they would say
and what we would hear
here where a degenerate mind ruled
but where also
hope primed the essence of the human race
and since then a wish and will for freedom
flew
took off into the blue sky ricocheting on the sea
in my country
thunder and storm reside in the belly of the elements
it groans and groans and groans
releasing hot air
at times it is not air but diarrhoea

Robben Island: at night I sleep
and toss and turn, toss and turn as the sea echoes and roars
seeking the spiritual hand of those who have been
those whose spirits were wrung by time
by cruelty
by loneliness
by bewilderment and wonder
when they asked –
why
why are the walls and the iron bars so wide
why are the doors and their keys so large
and the keys turn twice and thrice to lock
why
to keep the freedom of the breeze from itself
or
to stop the roar and rumble of the waves
who would
who can tell the ancestors what to do
who can break the particle of hope
who can bind the will to be free of a people?
I toss and turn

Robben Island: what have we learnt
what do we know now
when the cells and jails are empty
and echo ghosts only?

our address is
Robben Island
ask us we will tell you
Zizi
Madiba and his comrades left the cells
and you and we know our addresses
and the roaring seas sing of them
as the breeze whistles and whistles and whistles
and the earth spins on its miracle pin
if you go away
remember your home address

I
I will ask my beloved –
where

where must we reside in the early hours
in the purr and roar and chime
of the break of time
when the horizon yawns and is golden and mauve
when the breeze shimmers
when the spin of the earth sails the season into place
and when the blade of the wind and the breeze make us dream
we know our address
as the rain drizzle makes us stare the distances

Africa
here we are
we who people you
in shades which from blue to black to ginger to honey
dance with the light of the sun and the shades of the moon
and stars
or in the pitch dark of the night
in all seasons
out in your vast space
under your clear and blue skies which hover and watch
inside time which we carried and waded through
generation after generation after generation
we emerged without fail
like the day like night like seasons like time
are tempered and were tempered
in the long long moments of struggle
six centuries sixty decades of being doormats
these six hundred years of Africa fighting
should and must and shall open doors
crack as they do and dropping rust as if scraps
they shall beam the moonlight and the starlight and the sunlight
as we offer us to share the rewards of the struggle
and offer to be part of the human race
so all of us
black and white can be a gift to life
perhaps the human need

and the human interest may drive us all differently
to share
to divide all among us
is to threaten all life
perhaps we can set the tribe free
even the white ones
and the women of the land will enter
to bestow power over the land
as all barriers fall
and the democratic ones rise
to release the multitudes to bear their rights
as they would their obligations
the land must and shall be free
so if we go
all of us will remember our home address
to let the plenty of the earth
from its belly bring centuries of peace
to this earth which spins and spins and spins on its pin
need cannot be greed

Aushumato, you did sail
you who knew that all need the breeze but none can own it
you who asked that all must bear obligation
son who bore kings and chiefs
you the ancestor of the human race
help us free the African continent
we want to know
we want to plan
we want to work
we want to understand need and interest
and conquer them as you did the mighty ocean
hold counsel!
we are listening
to your voice which rings in the wind and the breeze
and in the noise of the waves

Aushumato
son of the old long land with ages in its heart
in its spirit
son of a land which is the tombstone of the oldest of life
here
we, as you know, try to make a home for all
with spirit
and with wounded flesh for having done so
yet
here, we hear your word
when you in your wisdom say –
for life to live
it must
be
lived

and those who come after you,
as our
time comes and must pass
we recall
for it is only in our lives where memory resides

at the end, when life sails and curls and disappears like thin clouds
your spirit
like the elements, must mould
and create
and make the space we live in a place for multitudes
to learn
and to know
that there is a particle in human life
in the spirit of human beings
which is invisible and incorrigible and hard

Motsoaledi, you passed on
often your life, like thunder, echoes in the space we live in
and Mlangeni
Mqhai and Khanyile
Sisulu and Mbeki
at the end, when life sails and curls and disappears like thin clouds,
your spirit
like the elements must too mould
and create
and make the space we live in a place for multitudes
to learn
and to know
that there is a particle in human life
in the spirit of human beings
which is invisible and incorrigible and hard
and it is the substance of this particle
which creates what is the treasure of life
and no large hammers can crush it
it flails in the wind and breeze
it sails between raindrops
this thing
it stays even in the corpses which men make
which float up in time
to tell tales
of greed and cruelty
of need gone mad
of interest propelled by avarice
where pharmaceuticals fly over the blue African sun
searching like vultures
ready to gobble the flesh of men women and children
who die
as HIV/AIDS ravages the continent and the earth

Oh Madiba
what must we, your sons and daughters, know
what must we learn
when the council of our ancestors sits together with the elements
presiding over our lives
what
what must we learn and know
African ancestors
hold counsel
we are listening and must make peace with you
Zizi stand firm and hear the voices
tsikitsikitsiki
tsikitsikitsikitsiki
tsa!
Linda, I said –
it is the seventh morning
let's go
time is waiting
come let us get to work

——

Mandela's Cell

I stood among a crowd
of tourists from abroad
and stared into his past.

A cage of bricks and bars
as gloomy and as cramped
as racial bias in the mind.

A bench, a gleam of bowl,
a stone-cold strip of floor
as make an ancient tomb

I could not hear the clang
shook from a gate of steel
that bigotry kept locked,

nor see a gaunt-faced man
fold up each dawn for years
the mat on which he'd dreamed.

Instead, far off, I heard
the cheering of the world
when he the era's Lazarus

walked out into the sun.
Around that unlocked gate,
that legacy's stark shrine,

the cameras flashed applause.

———

Glossary

1986 – The apartheid government implemented a national state of emergency in the run up to the 10th anniversary of the 1976 Soweto uprising

Aamblou – a traditional game

Achmad Timol – Communist party member who died in police custody after 'falling' from the 10th storey of John Vorster Square Police station in central Johannesburg in 1971

Adam Kok – Leader of the Griqua people in the 1860s

Adelaide Tambo – Wife of ANC president Oliver Tambo

Allan Boesak – Outspoken anti-apartheid cleric. He was disgraced for misuse of donor funding, charged and convicted of fraud

Amandla – meaning 'power'. Usually chanted as 'Amandla Awethu' – Power to the people

ama-Qwathi – the Qwathi people, a branch of the Xhosa people

Assegaai – short stabbing spear

Aushumato/Autshumato – Khoikhoi leader who acted as interpreter for English and Dutch colonizers in the Cape. Later imprisoned on Robben Island. He died in 1663

Azania – Africanist name for South Africa

Baasskap – assuming a state of authority based on race, (literally 'boss-ship', from Afrikaans)

Bafana Bafana – popular name for South Africa's national football team; means 'the boys'

Bantustan – region set aside by the apartheid government where ethnically distinct groups could set up their own 'government', such as Bophuthatswana and Transkei

Bioscope – cinema

Blouberg – beach across Table Bay from Table Mountain, in sight of Robben Island

Bloukrans – Blue Ridge, from Afrikaans

Boerewors – traditional Afrikaans sausage

Boipatong – place of massacre in 1992 when Inkatha supporters killed 45 ANC supporters. Apartheid security forces have been implicated as engineering the massacre.

Bootahlazy – Chief Mangosuthu Buthelezi, leader of the Zulu dominated Inkatha Freedom Party, now an opposition party in the South African government

BOSS – Bureau of State Security or the secret police

Botha, P.W. – became Prime Minister of South Africa in 1978. President 1983-1989. Known disparagingly as the 'Big Crocodile'

braai – barbeque, hence braaipap is maize meal porridge eaten with meat

Bucs – abbreviation of Bucanneers, popular name for leading football team Orlando Pirates

Cabral, Amilcar – revolutionary philosopher and guerrilla from Guinea Bissau and Cape Verde

Calon Lan and Gwlad y Gan – a hymn and a nationalist song both sung at rugby matches

Cape to Rio – annual yacht race from Cape Town to Rio de Janeiro, Brazil

Carcere duro ... Delenda apartheid – Latin, the rough translation of which means 'prison is hard... apartheid will wither'

Carter, Martin – Guyanese poet and politician

Casspir – armoured police vehicle, infamous for patrolling the townships

Chaka – 19th century Zulu chief

Charterist – person who believes in the principles laid out in the Freedom Charter formulated by the ANC in 1956

crc and nic – racially specific bodies which could legislate on minor matters only for their own race group, subject to White government approval

Clovelly – leafy suburb near Cape Town

Codesa – Congress for a Democratic South Africa, between the ANC and the apartheid government which negotiated the end of apartheid

Commissioner Street – main street through central Johannesburg

COSATU – Congress of South African Trade Unions

COSAW – Congress of South African Writers

Cronjé, Hansie – national cricket captain disgraced for match fixing. Died in a plane crash 2002

Dalibunga – name given to Mandela at the time of his circumcision, as a teenager

Dalindyebo, Jongintaba – Thembu chief who adopted Mandela on Mandela's father's death

Dassiebol – rock rabbit faeces but used to refer to a game

De Klerk, F.W. – last president of apartheid South Africa

Devil's Peak – part of Table Mountain overlooking Table Bay in Cape Town

Dingaan's Day – National holiday under apartheid celebrating the Boer victory over the Zulus at Blood River in 1836 where thousands of Zulus were massacred

Drakensberg – mountain range in central South Africa

Dube – suburb of Soweto, near Johannesburg

eGoli – alternative name for Johannesburg, meaning 'place of gold'

El – abbreviation in the United States for elevated railway

f.n. – semi-automatic rifle used by the South African police and security forces. Named for the Belgian company which manufactured them, Fabrique Nacionale

First, Ruth – South African anti-apartheid activist and Communist Party member, assassinated by a letter bomb while living in exile in Mozambique – not Zimbabwe as Soyinka's poem suggests

Fischer, Bram – lawyer who represented Mandela and his colleagues at the Rivonia trial

Fort – infamous prison in Johannesburg, now home of the country's constitutional court

Fratres – Latin for brotherhood

Goldberg, Dennis – ANC leader sentenced to life imprisonment at the same time as Mandela. He was released after serving 16 years

Goldreich, Arthur – ANC leader captured at Rivonia and one of Mandela's co-accused, but he escaped before the trial

Goniwe, Mathew – anti-apartheid activist and teacher from the Eastern Cape, assassinated by an apartheid hit squad in 1985

Goodison, Lorna – Jamaican poet

Guillen, Nicholas – Cuban poet

Hain, Peter – sports-crazy white South Africans loved to hate the UK Labour party activist who promoted the sports boycott against South Africa. Now UK's minister for Northern Ireland

Harris, John – member of the armed wing of the ANC, and chairman of the South African Non-Racial Olympic Committee. Hanged in 1965 at age 27 after being found guilty of terrorism, for having planted a bomb in Johannesburg central railway station. The only White person to be executed by the apartheid government for terrorism

Herero – a people from Namibia, victims of genocide by German colonisers

Herrenvolk – German for the chosen race, referring in this case to Afrikaaners

Hillbrow – suburb in central Johannesburg made up of high-rise apartment blocks

Hogmanay – Scottish new year festival

Jayne Cortez and Amiri Baraka – afro-American blues/jazz poets

Johannes Shabangu, David Moise, Bobby Tsotsobe – ANC guerrillas sentenced to death in South Africa in 1981 for their attack on a police station

Joseph, Helen – anti-apartheid activist, one of the 1956 treason trialists, and leader of the ANC Women's March in the same year. She died aged 87 in 1992

Kapitan – well-known Indian restaurant in Johannesburg, frequented by Mandela when he practised as a lawyer in the city

Kathrada, Ahmed – one of Mandela's co-accused at the Rivonia trial. He served 26 years as a political prisoner together with Mandela

Khonjwayo – an Mpondo chief

Kierie – stick with bulbous end, similar to night-stick

Kimathi, Dedan – Kenyan Mau-Mau freedom fighter executed by the British in 1957

Koeberg – nuclear power plant in the Western Cape, just north-east of Robben Island

Koevoet – special anti-terrorist police unit under apartheid (Afrikaans for 'crowbar')

Kruger, Paul – President of the South African Republic which went to war with Britain in 1899, known as the Anglo-Boer War

Kulukuthu – Xhosa word meaning isolation cell

Loftus Versveld – large sports stadium in Pretoria

Luthuli, Albert – ANC president from 1952-1967 and winner of the Nobel Peace prize in 1961

Makeba, Miriam – well known South African singer. Lived in exile after the South African government revoked her citizenship and right of return after she spoke out against apartheid at the UN in the early 1960s

Makulu team – literally 'Big team', referring to Mandela and his colleagues as prisoners held in high esteem by other political inmates

Malan, Verwoerd and Botha – all premiers of apartheid South Africa

Malelane – town in Mpumalanga province, in the east of South Africa

Matola – town adjacent to Maputo, Mozambique, intermittently raided by SA forces

Mayibuye i'Afrika – come back Africa

Mbeki, Govan – father of President Thabo Mbeki, and one of Mandela's co-accused at the Rivonia trial. He served 26 years as a political prisoner together with Mandela

Meadowlands – suburb of Soweto

Mfanafuthi – Johnny Mfanafuthi Makatini was director of the ANC's international affairs in exile at the time of his death in 1988. He 'nearly fainted' on seeing Mandela in Tanzania in 1962 when he thought the leader was in South Africa

Mhlaba, Raymond – one of the men sentenced with Nelson Mandela to life imprisonment in 1964. He died in February 2005

Milner, Lord Alfred – Governor of the Cape Colony who counselled for war against Kruger, which led to the Anglo-Boer War

Mlangeni, Andrew – one of Mandela's co-accused at the Rivonia trial. He served 26 years as a political prisoner together with Mandela

Moloise, Benjamin – ANC guerrilla executed by the apartheid government in 1985

Morena – lord

Motsoaledi, Andrew – one of Mandela's co-accused at the Rivonia trial. He served 26 years as a political prisoner together with Mandela

Mqhekezweni – capital of Thembuland, the royal residence of Chief Jongintaba Dalindyebo

Mtimkulu, Siphiwo – an Eastern Cape anti-apartheid activist murdered by Apartheid security forces at the same time as Mathew Goniwe

Mxenge, Griffiths and Victoria – lawyers (husband and wife) assassinated by an apartheid hit squad in 1985

Mzilikazi – Zulu chieftain who after the death of Shaka in 1820s fled Zululand to establish the kingdom of the Ndebele in modern-day Zimbabwe

neckbands – at the height of the township uprising in the 1980s crowds would place a tyre around the neck of suspected informers or those working for the state, douse it with petrol and set it alight

Nkosi sikelele iAfrika – 'God Bless Africa'; now the national anthem of South Africa, but sung as symbol of resistance

Nomzamo – Winnie Mandela's Xhosa name, from the noun 'ukuzama', connoting perseverance

North, Oliver – High ranking US military official helped organise illegal arms sales to Iran under the administration of Ronald Reagan, known as the Iran-Contra scandal

Nosekeni – Mandela's mother

Nyanga – traditional herbalist

Okigbo, Christopher – Nigerian poet who died in the civil war in Biafra

Onkgopotse, Mdluli, Mapetla – anti-apartheid activists murdered by the police forces

Orlando – suburb in the township of Soweto

Oshakati – town in northern Namibia which the SA Defence Force used as a staging post for the occupation of the area and incursions into Angola

Pass – refers to pass laws in which Blacks in South Africa were forced to carry an 'identity document' for entry into White areas

Percival, Lance – English comic actor and recording artist in the 1960s

Qokolweni – area in Transkei, South Africa

Qunu – Mandela's birth place

Ratel – armoured vehicle use by the apartheid security forces

Renamo – acronym for Mozambique National Resistance, South-African backed rebels who fought against the ruling Mozambican government. Now an opposition party in that country

Retief, Piet– Voortrekker who defeated Dingaan at Blood River in 1836 (see Voortrekker)

Rocklands and Grainger Bay – suburbs on the Atlantic seaboard of Cape Town, in sight of Robben Island

Rolihlahla – Mandela's middle name, meaning 'he who pulls along the severed bough'

S.B.s – Special Branch policemen

Sea Point – Cape Town suburb in sight of Robben Island

Section Twenty-Nine – Legislation of the apartheid government which allowed for indefinite detention without trial

Sisulu, Walter – one of the men sentenced with Nelson Mandela to life imprisonment in 1964

Sjambok – short, stiff whip frequently used by apartheid police to break up gatherings

Slovo, Joe – SA Communist party leader and husband of Ruth First. He went into exile after the party was banned in the 1950s. He died in1995

Smandje-Mandje – imminently

Sobukwe, Robert – Pan-Africanist Congress leader; the Sobukwe clause allowed the Minister of Justice to extend prison sentences for political prisoners

Sophiatown – Johannesburg suburb 'cleared' by the apartheid government in the 1950s to establish the white suburb of Triomf

Sun City – entertainment complex established in the bantustan of Bophuthatswana

Tambo, Oliver Reginald – ANC president who lived in exile for over three decades, returned to South Africa in 1991. He died in 1993 following a stroke

u'Tamsi, Tchikaya – surrealist Congolese poet

Transkei – homeland in South Africa during apartheid

Tsotsi – gangster, hoodlum

Turner, Rick – trade unionist assassinated by apartheid forces in the 1970s

Tweede Nuwe Jaar – Afrikaans meaning 'Second New Year'. The 2nd of January is traditionally taken as a public holiday in Cape Town, a tradition originating from the time of slavery

uBabwethu – our father

UDI – White Rhodesians declared a Unilateral Declaration of Independence on 11 November 1965, to perpetuate White minority rule in the British colony

Uhuru – Swahili for 'freedom'

Ukuhlabelela – isiZulu word meaning 'sing'

Umgungundlovu – Zulu capital

Umkhonto we Sizwe – Spear of the Nation, armed wing of the ANC

Unzima.... – words from a freedom song meaning 'It has been too long...'

Verwoerd, Hendrik – one of the architects of apartheid, became Prime Minister of South Africa in 1958

Voortrekker – Dutch inhabitants of the Cape colony who left en masse when slavery was outlawed in the 1830s and established the independent republics of Transvaal and Orange Free State. Predecessors of Afrikaners

Voortrekker Monument – built for the 100th anniversary of the defeat of the Zulu army under Dingaan at Blood River in 1836 by Piet Retief. Revered by many Afrikaners as nationalist symbol

Vorster, B.J. – became Prime Minister of South Africa in 1966 for twelve years

Webster, David – academic and anti-apartheid activist assassinated by an apartheid hit squad in 1989 for his sociological research in an area used by covert armed forces

Wolpe, Harold – Communist party member and lawyer who defended Mandela during the 1956 Treason trial. Arrested as part of the Rivonia trial but escaped into exile. Died 1996

Poet Biographies

Abialo, Benjamin (1959 -) was born in the Republic of Congo. He is a director in that country's Ministry of Finance. He is also a poet and journalist and participated in a 1987 international anti-apartheid literary symposium held in Brazzaville.

Adonis, [Ali Ahmad Said Asbar] (1930 -) is a Syrian poet, now living in France. He is one of the most important modern Arab poets. He was imprisoned in 1956 for his outspoken political views, after which he escaped to Lebanon. He lived in France after the civil war began in Lebanon in 1975. He has published four volumes of poetry.

Afrika, Tatamkhulu (1920 - 2002) was born in Egypt and taken to South Africa in 1923, orphaned, and raised by foster parents. In 1964, he reconverted to Islam and joined the resistance to apartheid. He was arrested in 1987 for terrorism. At the age of 17 he finished a first novel, *Broken Earth*. He has published five volumes of poetry and a novel.

Alexander, Elizabeth (1962 -) was born in Harlem, New York. She received a PhD in English from the University of Pennsylvania. Alexander's collections of poetry include *Antebellum Dream Book*, *Body of Life*, and *The Venus Hottentot*. She is a fellow at the Whitney Humanities Center at Yale University.

Anthony, Frank was a political prisoner on Robben Island in the 1980s.

Badinga, Mavoungou F.G. is a poet from the Congo (Brazzaville). He participated in a 1987 international anti-apartheid literary symposium held in Brazzaville.

Barlow, Mike (1942 -) is a English poet whose first collection, *Living on the Difference,* was overall winner of the Poetry Business Book and Pamphlet Competition 2003 and shortlisted for the 2005 Jerwood Aldeburgh Prize for best first collection. After a career as a probation officer, he now lives in Lancaster where he writes and practises as a visual artist.

Bissambou, Thomas is a poet from Congo (Brazzaville). He participated in a 1987 international anti-apartheid literary symposium held in Brazzaville.

Bontje, Jan (1947 -) was born Rotterdam, the Netherlands. He is a poet, columnist, songwriter and reviewer. In 1998 he published his first collection of haiku.

Brathwaite, Kamau (1930 -) was born in Bridgetown, Barbados. He received a PhD from the University of Sussex in 1968. From 1983 to 1991 he was Professor of Social and Cultural History at the University of the West Indies and became professor of Comparative Literature at New York University in 1993. As poet and cultural theorist he has transformed post-colonial Carribean verse with collections such a *The Arrivants: A New World Trilogy*.

Breytenbach, Breyten (1939 -) is one of South Africa's most prominent poets writing in Afrikaans. He was born in Bonnievale, South Africa. He left South Africa in 1960 and settled in Paris in 1962. Breytenbach returned to South Africa with a false passport in 1975, was arrested, charged under the Terrorism Act, and jailed for seven years. After his release he returned to Paris. His first volume of poetry was published in 1964.

Brirely, Roger (1929 -) was born in Zeerust, South Africa. Brirely is a pseudonym for the authoritative literary critic, editor, crime witer, retired professor of English and prolific poet. He lives in South Africa and is involved in encouraging aspirant poets and short story writers.

Brutus, Dennis (1924 -) was born in Zimbabwe. He attended the universities of Fort Hare and the Witwatersrand and taught in South African high schools. He helped secure South Africa's suspension from the Olympics in 1964 and expulsion in 1970. Trying to escape his ban to attend an Olympic meeting in Europe in 1963, he was arrested and subsequently sentenced to 18 months hard labour. Brutus was held captive on Robben Island. His first volume of poetry was published in Nigeria in 1962. He has published numerous volumes since then. He teaches at the University of Pittsburgh in the US.

Bryer, Lynne (1946-1994) was born and educated in the Eastern Cape, where she completed her MA in English at Rhodes University in 1969. In 1991 she was awarded the AA life Vita/Arthur Nortje poetry award.

Busia, Abena P.A is a Ghanian poet and academic at Rutgers University in the USA.

Cashdan, Liz (1928 -) was born in London and lives in Sheffield, where she teaches creative writing at Sheffield University Institute of LifeLong Learning. She is the editor of the UK's National Association of *Writers in Education* journal. Her collection of poetry, *Pictures from Exhibitions*, contains several poems based on her experiences in South Africa.

Clark, J.P. [John Pepper Clark-Bekederemo] (1935 -) was born in Nigeria. He obtained an English degree from University College, Ibadan. After a period in the USA at Princeton University he became editor of the influential literary magazine *Black Orpheus* and became Professor of English at the University of Lagos. He has since retired. His numerous volumes of poetry include *A Reed in the Tide*.

Clayton, Cherry (1943 -) taught English at the University of Witwatersrand and Rand Afrikaans University in Johannesburg. She has published poetry and short stories in literary journals in South Africa, England and Canada. Her first poetry collection, *Leaving Home*, was awarded the CNA prize for best debut volume. She lives in Canada.

Craveirinha, José (1922-2003) was born in Maputo, Mozambique. As a journalist, Craveirinha contributed to numerous Mozambican magazines and newspapers. He was imprisoned from 1965 to 1969 for his membership of the liberation movement Frelimo. He continued to work as a journalist after independence in 1975. He was awarded the Prémio Camões, the world's highest honour for Lusophone literature, in 1991. His first volume of poetry was published in the 1960s and he continued to publish poems until his death.

Cronin, Jeremy (1949 -) was a lecturer in political science at the University of Cape Town until his imprisonment in 1976 on charges of terrorism. He served seven years in Pretoria prison. He is now an MP of the African National Congress and deputy secretary-general of the South African Communist Party. *Inside*, a collection of his poetry, was published in South Africa in 1986.

d'Almedia, Armindo Vaz is a sociologist and was President of São Tomé and Principe from 1995-1996. A volume of his poetry has been published in Portugal.

Davis, Karen lives in Louisville, Kentucky. She is a member of Voices in the Wind: An African-American Women's Literary Series. Her previous poems have been included in *MandelAmandla* and *The Dark Woods I Cross*.

Dederick, Robert (1919-1983) was born in Manchester, England and was a solicitor by profession. He came to South Africa during the Second World War and settled in Cape Town after the war. His poetry was widely published in South African literary magazines and he published two volumes of poetry.

Dhamac, Maxamed Xaashi 'Gaarriye' (1949 -) was born in Hargeysa, Somalia. From the 1970s onwards, he has been one of the most important Somali poets, composing on a variety of topics from nuclear weapons to Nelson Mandela. He writes in Somali, and was a leading poet in a 2005 UK tour of world poets arranged by The Poetry Translation Centre of the University of London's School of Oriental and African Studies.

Edwards, Emyr (1931-) was born in Aberystwyth and educated at the University of Wales. He worked as a documentary producer and lecturer. He has written over 50 commissioned and performed plays and musicals and is the founder of Urdd Welsh National Theatre Company. He has published twenty books on drama and theatre. Poems published in English and Welsh in magazines and poetry collections, including *Triumph House* and *Poets against Apartheid*.

February, Vernon (1938-2002) was born in Somerset-West, South Africa. He worked at the African Studies Centre in Leiden, the Netherlands, for more than 30 years before returning to South Africa in 2002. From 1990 he was a guest lecturer in the Afrikaans Department at the University of the Western Cape, South Africa. He published poems in Afrikaans and in English including collections entitled *O Snotverdriet* and *Spectre de la Rose*.

Feinberg, Barry (1938 -) was born in Germiston, South Africa. He went into exile to London in 1961. He edited an anthology of anti-apartheid poetry entitled *Poets to the People*. His poetry was published in *Gardens of Struggle*. He lives in Cape Town.

Fourie, Gerrit (1947 -) was educated at Rhodes University in South Africa. He published several poems in South African literary journals and magazines. He was head of South Africa's Road Safety Council in the late 1970s. A collection of his poetry *Bokas en ondertoon* was published in 1976.

Galvin, Patrick (1927 -) was born in Cork, Ireland. In the 1950s he began writing poetry. His first book of poetry was *Heart of Grace* (1959). He moved back to Dublin in 1962, as his first play, *And Him Stretched*, was staged in London. *Song for a Poor Boy*, the first of three volumes of memoirs appeared in 1990. He lives in Cork.

Golden is a South African whose poem was published in *MandelAmandla* (1989).

Gottschalk, Keith (1946 -) works in the Political Studies Department at the University of the Western Cape. He has given over one hundred performances of his poems, and has had more than 100 poems published in magazines such as *New Coin, New Contrast, Phoebe, Staffrider* and *Agenda*. His first collection *Emergency Poems* was published in 1992. During the 1980s Keith served on the executive of the Congress of South African Writers. Today he is Western Cape chair of the South African Writers' Association.

Gwala, Mafika (1946 -) was born in KwaZulu-Natal and brought up in Durban. He has worked as a secondary school teacher, legal clerk, factory worker, publications researcher, and industrial relations officer. He has also lived in England, where he did research on adult education at the University of Manchester. He has published two volumes of verse: *Yakhal'inkomo* and *No More Lullabies*, as well as short stories and essays.

Hadfield, Jen (1978 -) works as writer in residence for the Shetland Arts Trust. She is learning folksongs on the mandolin and taking photographs. Her collection *Almanacs* was published in 2005. She received an Eric Gregory Award in 2003.

Heaney, Seamus (1939 -) was born in County Derry in Northern Ireland. He was awarded the Nobel Prize for literature in 1995. He lived in Belfast from 1957 to 1972. Heaney's poems first came to public attention in the mid-1960s when he was active as one of a group of poets who were subsequently recognised as constituting something of a 'Northern School' within Irish writing. He has been the recipient of several honorary degrees.

Henderson, Hamish (1919-2002) was born in Blairgowrie, Scotland. He studied modern languages at Cambridge. As a visiting student in Germany he acted as a courier for a Quaker network which helped refugees to escape the Nazi regime. He worked at the School of Scottish Studies in the University of Edinburgh. In 1983 he refused an OBE in protest at the nuclear arms policy of the Thatcher government.

Hirson, Denis (1951 -) was born in Cambridge, England, of South African parents. He lived in South Africa from 1952 to 1973, the year in which his father, who had been a political prisoner for nine years, was released. Since 1975 he has lived and worked in France. He has written three books, all mosaics of memory, has edited two anthologies of South African poems and short stories.

Hoho, Daluxolo lives in Cape Town, and worked for the Medical Research Council investigating the uses of traditional medicines.

Horn, Peter (1934 -) was born in Germany and educated there and in South Africa. He is Professor of German at the University of Cape Town. He has published six volumes of poetry and two volumes of essays on South African poetry.

Horwitz, Allan Kolski (1952 -) grew up and studied in Cape Town. He left South Africa in 1974, living in Middle East, Europe and North America before returning in 1986. He lives in Johannesburg and serves on the editorial board of Botsotso, a publishing collective. He has published a volume of poetry, *Call from the Free State* and a collection of short fiction, *Uncommon Ground*.

Ikeme, Jekwu is an environmental economist, poet and public affairs commentator. He obtained his MSc and PhD from Oxford and De Montfort universities respectively in the United Kingdom. He has had poems featured in *Okike* and *ANA Review* – the official Journal of Association of Nigerian Authors.

Innocent, Durumurali is a poet from Rwanda. He participated in a 1987 international anti-apartheid literary symposium held in Brazzaville.

Johennesse, Fhazel (1956 -) was born in Johannesburg. Of the *Rainmaker* (in which 'bombs' first appeared) he says: "I have been told that writing poetry about being black is troublemaking. But this is so wrong. My writing is a confirmation of my humanitiy, a celebration of my blackness."

Johnson, Lynton Kwesi (1952 -) was born in Chapelton, Jamaica. He moved to London in 1963 and went on to read Sociology at Goldsmiths College, University of London. He joined the Black Panther movement in 1970, organising a poetry workshop and working with Rasta Love, a group of poets and percussionists. He is widely regarded as the father of 'dub poetry', a term he coined to describe the way a number of reggae DJs blended music and verse. He founded LKJ Records and lives in Brixton, south London.

Kgositsile, Keorapetse (1938 -) taught for many years at the University of Dar es Salaam, the University of Nairobi, Kenya, and the University of Gaborone, Botswana. He spent most of the 1960s in political exile all over the world, including the USA and Botswana. His works include *Spirits Unchained*, *For Melba*, *My Name is Afrika*, *The Present Is a Dangerous Place to Live*, *Places and Bloodstains*, *The Word Is Here*, and *When the Clouds Clear*. He returned to South Africa in the early 1990s and is now an adviser to the Minister of Arts and Culture.

de Kok, Ingrid (1951 -) was born in the western Transvaal, South Africa. She obtained an MA in English in 1984, the year in which she returned to South Africa from Canada. Since 1988 she has been professor at the Centre of Extra-Mural Studies at the University of Cape Town. Her poetry has been widely published.

Kunene, Mazisi (1930 -) lives in KwaZulu-Natal, South Africa. Kunene studied at the University of Natal, and won the Bantu Literary Competition Award in 1956. He left South Africa in 1959, taught in Lesotho, and became Professor of African Literature and Language at the University of California in Los Angeles. With the publication of *Emperor Shaka the Great* and *Anthem of the Decades* Kunene earned critical as well as popular recognition. He was South Africa's first Poet Laureate.

Leggott, Michele (1956 -) was born in Stratford, Taranaki, New Zealand and educated at New Plymouth GHS and University of Canterbury. She completed a PhD at the University of British Columbia in Canada in 1985. She returned to a lectureship at the University of Auckland. Her poems appeared in periodicals and her third book *DIA* won the New Zealand Book Award for Poetry.

Lewis, Emyr is a Welsh poet.

Mabuza, Lindiwe (1938 -) was born in Newcastle, Kwa-Zulu Natal, South Africa. She began her career in 1962 teaching English and Zulu Literature in Swaziland. From 1979 to 1994 she represented the ANC in Scandinavian countries and the USA. In 1994 she was elected to South Africa's first democratic parliament. She became South African High Commissioner to the United Kingdom in 2001. Her poetry collections include *Malibongwe*, *Letter to Letta*, *Africa to me* and *Voices that Lead*.

MacKay Langa, Ilva (1952 -) completed her schooling at Uitenhage High School in South Africa. In 1977 she left South Africa and obtained political asylum in the United Kingdom where she worked in the Anti-Apartheid Movement. She has worked in the South African government since 1995, and is currently Deputy Chief Executive Officer in the Government Communication and Information Services.

Madhubuti, Haki R [Donald Luther Lee] (1942 -) was born in Little Rock, Arkansas, USA. He has worked as poet, publisher, editor and educator. He has published 24 books of poetry and non-fiction. He is Professor, founder and Director Emeritus of the Gwendolyn Brooks Center for Black Literature and Creative Writing and director of the Master of Fine Arts in Creative Writing Program at Chicago State University.

Magaia, Albino (1947 -) was born in Maputo, Mozambique. He works as a journalist and has been director of the weekly news magazine *Tempo*. He served as secretary-general for the Association of Mozambican writers in the early 1990s. He has published two novels and a collection of poetry.

Maimona, João (1955 -) was born in the Angolan province of Uige. After a living in exile in Zaire for 15 years before his country's independence in 1975, he settled in Huambo where he worked as a veterinary surgeon. His poetry has appeared in numerous journals in Angola and internationally. He is a member of the Union of Angolan Writers and a member of the parliament of Angola.

Mamonsono, Leopold Pindy is a poet from the Congo. He participated in a 1987 international anti-apartheid literary symposium held in Brazzaville.

Mandela-Hlongwane, Zindziswa [Zindzi] (1961 -) is the youngest daughter of Nelson and Winnie Mandela. She was 18 months old when her father was sent to prison, and 14 when she first saw him again on Robben Island. In 1985, Zindzi made headlines when she read aloud her father's response to the government's conditional release offer. She works in Johannesburg.

Mann, Chris works at the Institute for the Study of English in Africa in Grahamstown after more than a decade in rural and peri-urban development at The Valley Trust on the outskirts of Durban. His recent work includes *South Africans: A series of portrait poems*.

Maracle, Lee (1950 -) of Salish and Cree ancestry, a member of the Stoloh nation, was born in North Vancouver, British Colombia, Canada. She is the traditional cultural director of The Centre for Indigenous Theatre and the visiting Professor of Canadian Culture at Western Washington University.

Matshikiza, John (1954 -) was born in Johannesburg, South Africa, and grew up in Lusaka and London, where he trained in drama and worked as an actor, writer and director. He returned to South Africa in 1991, and has since been writing and working in theatre, film and television. A joint collection of columns written by his father, Todd Matshikiza, and himself, *With the Lid Off*, was published in 2000.

Mattera, Don (1935 -) poet, autobiographer, and short-story writer, was born in Western Native Township, Johannesburg and was a founding member of the Black Consciousness movement. His publications include *Azanian Love Song*, a book of poems that won a PEN award in 1983. He continues to write as well as working with street children in the Eldorado Park community in South Africa.

Maunick, Edouard (1931 -) trained as a school teacher and a librarian. He published his first volume of poetry in Port Louis, Mauritius. Apart from his career as poet and writer he also worked for Unesco. After his retirement he becamed Mauritian ambassador to the new South Africa. He lives in Pretoria.

Mayor Zaragoza, Federico (1934 -) was born in Barcelona, Spain. He holds a PhD in pharmacy from the Universidad Computense de Madrid. He became Spain's minister of education and science in 1981. In 1987, he was elected Director-General of Unesco. In 1999 he returned to Spain and created the Fundación Cultura de Paz, of which he is chairman. In addition to his numerous scientific publications, he has published four books of poetry.

Momen, Sarafat Ibn [Shumon] (1979 - 1992) grew up in London and died of illnesses related to his struggle with leukemia. He published his own poems and won first prize for his efforts at Wanstead Library, London, for two consecutive years.

Morejon, Nancy (1944 -) was born in Havana, Cuba. She published her first collection of poems *Mutismos* in 1962. She went on to Havana University, where she studied French. She has been editor of the Union of Cuban Writers and Artists and since the 1980s she has published a new collection of poems almost annually. From 1986 to 1993 and again from 2000 she has been head of the Cuban research centre at the Casa de las Americas in Havana. In 2001 she received the Cuban national prize for literature.

Motion, Andrew (1952 -) became England's Poet Laureate in 1999. He read English at University College, Oxford and taught English at the University of Hull. He is a Fellow of the Royal Society of Literature and has been chairman of the Arts Council of England's Literature Panel since 1996. His poetry collections include *Independence*; *Secret Narratives*; *Dangerous Play: Poems 1974-1984*, *Natural Causes*, *The Price of Everything*; *Salt Water and Selected Poems 1976-1997*. He lives in London.

Mtshali, Oswald (1940 -) was born in KwaZulu-Natal, South Africa. He was working as a messenger in Soweto when he published his first volume of poetry *Sounds of a Cowhide Drum* in 1971. Mtshali left for the USA to study creative writing and education. He is now Adjunct Professor at the New York City College of Technology where he teaches African folklore and modern African history.

Nicol, David (1962 -) was born in Dundee, Scotland. He spent part of his childhood in South Africa. He was educated at the Universities of Strathclyde and Stirling and is now a writer and part-time tutor at the Royal Scottish Academy of Music and Drama. His first novel, *The Fundamentals of New Caledonia*, was published in 2003.

Niehaus, Carl (1959 -) was born in Zeerust, South Africa. He attended the Rand Afrikaans University in Johannesburg where he started a preparatory degree in theology. He was expelled from university for having put up posters on the campus calling for equal non-racial education and the release of Nelson Mandela. In 1983 he received a 15 year sentence for treason. He served as an ANC MP and worked for the Gauteng Economic Development Agency.

Nortje, Arthur (1942-1970) was born in Oudtshoorn and educated in Port Elizabeth, where he was taught by the writer Dennis Brutus, University College of the Western Cape, and Oxford University. In 1967 he emigrated to Canada but returned to Oxford in 1970, where he committed suicide shortly afterwards. His poems were published posthumously in the collections *Dead Roots* and *Lonely Against the Light*.

Ojo-Ade, Femi (1943 -) was born and raised in Nigeria. He studied in Senegal, Canada, Spain, and France. He obtained his PhD in French and Francophone literature at the University of Toronto in 1975. He is professor of French and Francophone Studies at St. Mary's College of Maryland, USA. His latest books include *Death of a Myth: critical Essays on Nigeria*, and the novel, *The Almond Tree*.

Oliphant, Andries Walter (1955 -) is a writer, academic and arts and culture policy developer. He has been involved in independent publishing in South Africa as an editor for Ravan Press and Staffrider Magazine and later as general editor of the Publishing House of the Congress of South African Writers. He played a leading role in the development of arts, culture and media policies for a democratic South Africa as chairperson of the National Arts Coalition and the government's Arts and Culture Task Group. He is a lecturer in the Literary Theory department at the University of South Africa and chairs the Arts and Culture Trust.

Press, Karen (1956 -) was born in Cape Town, South Africa. She works as a freelance editor and writer, and is involved in an initiative to set up a national advice and information support service for South African writers, The Writers' Network. Press has published seven collections of poetry and has also written textbooks and other education materials. In 1987 she co-founded the publishing collective Buchu Books. Her poetry has appeared in various anthologies

Rampolokeng, Lesego (1965 -) was born in Orlando West, Soweto. He performed his lyrics in classrooms and lecture theatres. He has published five volumes of poetry. In 1990 *Horns for Hondo*, his first anthology of poems, was published. *End Beginnings* with the Kalahari Surfers, a South African band, was published in 1993. Rampolokeng performs in Africa, Europe and the USA. His poems have also been translated into German by Thomas Brückner. He has also published a novel, *Blackheart*.

Rocha, Jofre [pseudonym of Roberto de Almeida] (1941 -) was born in Cachimane, Angola. After school he joined the armed struggle against Portuguese colonialism. After independence in 1975 he held various ministerial posts and is now chairman of Angola's National Assembly. He has published a number of anthologies of poetry.

Salaam, Kalamu ya (1947 -) was born Vallery Ferdinand III in New Orleans, Louisiana. He is a professional editor/writer, filmmaker, producer and arts administrator. He is the founder and director of NOMMO Literary Society, a New Orleans-based Black writers workshop and has published a number of poetry collections.

Samuels, Mark Anthony was born in East London. He lived in Stevenage, England.

Seakhoa, Morakabe 'Raks' (1959 -) was regional co-ordinator and secretary general of the Congress of South African Writers from 1988 to 1997. He was Convenor of the South African Writers' Federation and served as the founding chairperson of the Southern African Writers' Council. Until 2000, he was a Convenor of the Arts, Culture & Heritage Commission of the South African Chapter of the African Renaissance. He has been involved in most aspects of arts and culture since his release from a five-year incarceration on Robben Island (1979-1984). He now heads the wRite Associates, a communications agency.

Sepamla, Sipho (1932 -) was born in West Rand Consolidated Mines Township outside Krugersdorp, near Johannesburg, and trained as a teacher at Pretoria Normal College. He has published six collections of poetry and several novels. In 1978 Sepamla was instrumental in establishing the Fuba Academy of Arts in South Africa. He has served on the Arts and Culture Task Group, a think-tank that advises government on artistic and cultural issues.

Serote, Mongane Wally (1944 -) was born in Sophiatown and brought up in Alexandra, a black township near Johannesburg. He worked as a journalist before going to the USA where he gained a master's degree in creative writing at Columbia University. He remained in exile until 1990 and in 1994 became an ANC member of parliament. He chairs the parliamentary committee on arts, culture, science, and technology.

Shakur, Tupac (1971 - 1996) was born in Brooklyn, New York. Early in his life, he moved to Baltimore, Maryland, where he attended The Baltimore School for the Performing Arts. His public life began when he joined the rap group, digital underground, first as a tour dancer, then as a rapper. He released his first solo album *2pacalypes Now*. He recorded numerous albums, including *Brenda's Got A Baby*, *Keep Ya Head Up* and *Strictly for my Niggaz*. He was shot dead by unknown gunmen. Much of what happened on the night of his death remains a mystery.

Shange, Ntozake (1948 -) was born in Trenton, New Jersey. She obtained a master's degree in American Studies in 1973 from the University of Southern California, Los Angeles. Her books of poetry include *Ridin' the Moon in Texas: Word Paintings*, *From Okra to Greens*, *A Daughter's Geography*, *Nappy Edges*, *Natural Disasters and Other Festive Occasions*, and *Melissa & Smith*. She has written numerous plays including *For colored girls who have considered suicide/when the rainbow is enuf*.

Sitole, Bongani is an oral poet who lives near Umtata, in the Eastern Cape, South Africa. He worked as a research assistant at the University of Transkei and is now retired.

Smith, Michael (1954 - 1984) was born in Jones Town, Jamaica, West Indies. He was educated at Kingston College and the St. George's College Extension School. In 1981, he represented Jamaica in Venezuela at the World Festival Of Youth. Smith appeared on the BBC television series *Ebony*, performing 'Long Time' and 'Give Me Little Dub Music'. In 1982, he released his debut album and performed at Unesco function in Paris. In 1983, he returned to Jamaica. Smith was stoned to death following an altercation at a political rally.

Sole Kelwyn (1951 -) is associate professor in English at the University of Cape Town, South Africa. He has won national and international awards for his poetry, and is developing ties with US universities with a view to further contributions to the teaching of creative writing in the department. His poetry collections include *The Blood of Our Silence* and *Projections in the Past Tense*.

Soyinka, Wole (1934 -) was born near Ibadan in western Nigeria. He received his doctorate from the University of Leeds in 1973. From 1958 until 1959 he was a dramaturgist at the Royal Court Theatre in London. He taught drama and literature at various universities in Ibadan, Lagos, and Ife, where, since 1975, he has been Professor of comparative literature. During the civil war in Nigeria, Soyinka appealed in an article for ceasefire for which he was arrested in 1967 and was held as political prisoner until 1969. Soyinka has published about 20 works of drama, novels and poetry. He received Nobel Prize for literature in 1986.

Tieco, Diarra B. is a poet from France. He participated in a 1987 international anti-apartheid literary symposium held in Brazzaville, Congo.

Thani is the pseudonym of Jonathan de Vries, a film maker who lives in Johannesburg.

Vasconcelos, Leite de (1944-1997) was born in Arcos de Valdevez, Portugal, but lived in Mozambique and came to be known as one of its leading intellectuals. He was a radio journalist, serving as director-general of Radio Mozambique, as well as poet and playwright. A collection of his newspaper columns *Pela Boca Morre o Peixe* was published posthumously.

we Jojo, Nogqaza is from Cape Town, South Africa.

Williams, Mary Ann is from Columbus, Ohio.

Zephaniah, Benjamin (1958 -) grew up in Jamaica and Birmingham, England. He is a poet, novelist and playwright. He has been Creative Artist in Residence at Cambridge University. He holds a number of honorary doctorates and in 1998 was appointed to the National Advisory Committee on Creative and Cultural Education to advise on the place of music and art in education. In 2003 Zephaniah refused an OBE.

Translators' Biographies

Bartlett, Richard (1965 -) grew up in South Africa. He has an MA in African Literature from the University of Durban-Westville and has translated works of Mozambican literature into English and edited *Short Stories from Mozambique*. He works as a journalist in London and edits the *African Review of Books*.

Dewar, Michael C. (1979 -) was born in Wegberg, Germany. He attended schools in Dorset and West Sussex, before reading philosophy and Spanish at King's College London and Birmingham Universities. He is a student member of the Institute of Linguists.

Harsent, David was born in Devonshire and has published nine collections of poetry. His most recent, *Legion* was shortlisted for the Forward Prize. His translation work includes the Bosnian poet Goran Simic, most notably his versions of *Sprinting From the Graveyard*.

Mchunu, Vusi was editor of Isivivane African literary-cultural Journal; Berlin, West Germany, before the end of apartheid. He has published a collection of poetry and essays. He works in Johannesburg as a heritage business manager and is a member of the board of South Africa's Arts and Culture Trust.

Mitras, Luis is a South African based in Lisbon, Portugal. He teaches for the University of Maryland University College (European Divison). He has published academic papers on Lusophone literature.

Orwin, Martin (1963 -) studied Arabic and Amharic, and has a PhD in the phonology of Somali. Since 1992 he has been a lecturer in Somali and Amharic at SOAS, London. He has published articles on Somali language and poetry and *Colloquial Somali*, a language learners' textbook. He has done research in the Horn of Africa, with ongoing research interests in the metrics of Somali poetry.

Reckless, Ann grew up in the Snowdonia region of Wales and is now a journalist based in London.

Index by poet

Acknowledgements

The editor and publishers of this book have made considerable effort to contact all rights holders, whether the poets themselves or their publishers. This has been difficult in some cases: poets are deceased and their heirs are untraceable; publishing houses have ceased to exist or have merged; poets have moved and their whereabouts are unknown. The editor and publishers wish sincerely to thank all those who granted permission and all those who assisted in our search by providing leads. We welcome any further information that anyone is able to provide.

Thanks are due to the following:
the individual poets who kindly granted permission – Benjamin Abialo, Adonis, Mike Barlow, Dennis Brutus, Abena P.A. Busia, Liz Cashdan, Jeremy Cronin, Karen Davis, Emyr Edwards, Patrick Galvin, Keith Gottschalk, Mafika Gwala, Jen Hadfield, Denis Hirson, Peter Horn, Allan Kolski Horwitz, 'Bro Willie' Kgositsile, Ingrid de Kok, Emyr Lewis, Lindiwe Mabuza, Ilva Mackay, Albino Magaia, Zindzi Mandela, Chris Mann, John Matshikiza, Don Mattera, Federico Mayor, Sandile Ngidi, David Nicol, Femi Ojo-Ade, Andries Oliphant, Karen Press, Lesego Rampolokeng, Kalamu ya Salaam, Morakabe Seakhoa, Sipho Sepamla, Kelwyn Sole and Jonathan de Vries; the widow of Hamish Henderson, the daughters of Robert Dederick and Lynne Bryer and the families of Shumon Momen and José Craveirinha; South Africa's National English Literary Museum for the poem by Tatamkhulu Afrika; Bloodaxe Books for the poems by Kamau Brathwaite and Benjamin Zephaniah; Calder Publications for the poem by Breyten Breytenbach; Theytus Books for the poem by Lee Maracle; the Poetry Translation Centre of London University's School of Oriental and African Studies for the poem by Maxamed Xaashi Dhamac; trustees of the Mazisi Kunene Foundation, and Vusi Mchunu for Mazisi Kunene's poem; Faber and Faber and Farrar, Straus and Giroux for the poem by Seamus Heaney; Auckland University Press for the poem by Michele Leggott; the Associação dos Escritores Moçambicanos for poem by Leite de Vasconcelos; the União dos Escritores Angolanos for the poems by Jofre Rocha and João Maimona; Protea Book House for the poem by Edouard Maunick; Mango Publishing for the poem by Nancy Morejón; PFD for the poem by Andrew Motion; LKJ Music Publishers for the poem by Linton Kwesi Johnson; Kwela Books for the poem by Wally Mongane Serote; and Wole Soyinka for his poems which originally appeared in *Selected Poems* and are reprinted with permission of Melanie Jackson Agency, LLC.